J.B. HIXSON

Weekly Words of Life

52 Devotionals to Warm your Heart and Strengthen your Faith

First published by Not By Works, Inc. 2020

Copyright © 2020 by J.B. Hixson

All rights reserved. No part of this publication may be reproduced, stored or transmitted in any form or by any means, electronic, mechanical, photocopying, recording, scanning, or otherwise without written permission from the publisher. It is illegal to copy this book, post it to a website, or distribute it by any other means without permission.

All Scripture quotations taken from the New King James Version unless otherwise indicated.

Some portions of this book have been adapted from the author's previous works including articles, blogs, sermons, books, and DVDs.

Cover photo of Glacier National Park by J. B. Hixson (c) 2019

First edition

ISBN: 979-8-9858535-1-3

This book was professionally typeset on Reedsy. Find out more at reedsy.com

DEDICATION
To my granddaughter Zoe.
May she grow up to see wondrous things from God's Word.

"Open my eyes, that I may see wondrous things from Your law."
(Psalm 119:18)

Sing them over again to me,
Wonderful words of life.
Let me more of their beauty see,
Wonderful words of life.
Words of life and beauty,
Teach me faith and duty.

Sweetly echo the gospel call,
Wonderful words of life.
Offer pardon and peace to all,
Wonderful words of life;
Jesus, only Savior,
Sanctify forever.

Beautiful words, wonderful words,
Wonderful words of life.
Beautiful words, wonderful words,
Wonderful words of life.

- P. P. Bliss (1874)

Contents

Preface		iv
1	New Beginnings	1
2	Never Look Back?	3
3	Things That Matter…Things That Don't	7
4	Life Is Not a Game of "Go Fish!"	9
5	The Counsel of God's Word	13
6	True Love	17
7	Turn Down the Volume So You Can Hear!	21
8	Are Monsters Afraid of You?	25
9	Only God Is Great	29
10	The Amazing Race	33
11	What Matters Most	37
12	Cloudy Medicine	41
13	Warm on the Inside	45
14	Don't Just Do Something, Stand There!	49
15	Identity Crisis	53
16	All Is Forgiven	57
17	Reign, Reign, Go Away!	61
18	Backseat Driver	65
19	Surviving the Culture of Now	69
20	Look for the Light	73
21	The Golden Key	77
22	God, Glory, and Sleepy Hollow	81
23	There Is No Comparison	85

24	Leggo My Ego!	89
25	A Few Good Fools	91
26	The Calcium of the Soul	95
27	Unshakable Faith	97
28	Mending a Broken Heart	101
29	Lord Please Send More Bears!	105
30	Old Habits Die Hard	109
31	Planks, Specks, and Self-Righteous Prigs!	113
32	Slow Down and Save Time	117
33	A Measure of Assurance	121
34	Where Do You Live?	125
35	Doctrine Is Dead	129
36	Bright Lights and Other Distractions	133
37	Fruit Inspectors	135
38	Good, Better, Best	139
39	Godly Fear	141
40	Whose Neighbor Are You?	145
41	Hope in Exile	149
42	One Nation Under God	151
43	Things Are Not Always as They Appear	155
44	Elusive Peace	159
45	Believe It or Not	163
46	Thankful for the Little Things	165
47	The Insanity of Ingratitude	169
48	Spiritual Somnambulism	175
49	A Forever Savior	179
50	God in the Midst	183
51	A Truly White Christmas	187
52	New Life in Christ	191
	Afterword	195
	About the Author	199

Also by J.B. Hixson

Preface

When I was in junior high, I had the privilege of attending summer youth camps at Word of Life in Schroon Lake, New York. My time at *Word of Life* had a meaningful influence on me, even as a young boy. I grew up in a Bible-believing, Christian home, and I trusted Christ for salvation at the age of six. My parents taught me and my sisters to value and respect the Word of God. We attended Bible-teaching churches, and, for many years, we participated in an at-home Bible memory program called Bible Memory Association (BMA). The Bible was central in our home. Yet it was at *Word of Life* that I recall first learning to have a daily quiet time. I still have my old Word of Life Quiet Time diaries in a box of keepsakes somewhere.

Word of Life camp is nestled among the trees on a 49-acre island in the middle of Schroon Lake in upstate New York. It is a tranquil setting and a great place to grow closer to the Lord. I remember vividly the daily routine at camp. Each morning began with campers gathering in groups of eight to ten for devotional time. We sat in a circle outside, with small groups of campers sprinkling the picturesque campus. I had my *Scofield Reference Bible* on my lap. A group leader, usually a camp counselor, read from Scripture and shared a few words. There was a daily Bible verse to memorize—something that came easily to me thanks to the BMA program we used in our home. After the small group meeting, campers were encouraged to find a solitary place, read the day's Scripture passage, and write down some thoughts in our Quiet Time diaries.

In my mind, I have a detailed recollection of a particular morning when our group leader was not one of the typical, college-aged camp counselors, but an older gentleman. I had seen him frequently around the camp. He had white hair and appeared to be one of the camp's administrators. After all these years, that one devotional meeting, with the kind, old gentleman, still stands out in my mind. The man with white hair exuded wisdom, and he seemed to really believe what he was saying. He loved God's Word and wanted me and the other campers to do the same. Normally at these morning devotionals, it was hard for me to avoid the distraction of other outdoor activities going on within my line of sight. In this case, however, I found myself fixated on every word this man said. He taught us how to handle the Word of God correctly; to "cut straight." (2 Timothy 2:15)

It was many years later before I realized that I and the other children in our small group had been taught on that bright summer morning by a great stalwart of the faith, John Von Casper Wyrtzen. "Jack," as his friends and colleagues knew him, was not just a camp administrator, as I had presumed. He was the founder of *Word of Life*. Jack Wyrtzen died on April 17, 1996, the same day one of my children was born. I am forever indebted to him and *Word of Life* camps for helping to undergird what I had learned at home; namely, that God's Word is the only standard for our beliefs, attitudes, and practices. "Your word is a lamp to my feet and a light to my path." (Psalm 119:105)

Because those weeks at *Word of Life* hold such a special place in my heart to this day, I decided to title this book *Weekly Words of Life*. It contains a collection of devotionals I have written over the past thirty years, each one based upon a different passage of Scripture. Following the pattern that I learned more than forty years ago at summer camp, I interact with the selected passage in each devotional and apply it to everyday life. Along the way I share anecdotes, stories, and illustrations from my own experiences that I hope will warm your heart and strengthen your faith.

In keeping with the title *Weekly Words of Life*, I selected one devotional for each of the fifty-two weeks of the year. The goal is for you to read one devotional at the beginning of each week, and let the Word dwell in you richly throughout that week (Colossians 3:16). I still remember the first Bible verse I memorized at one of those *Word of Life* summer camps as a young boy. "That you may walk worthy of the Lord, fully pleasing Him, being fruitful in every good work and increasing in the knowledge of God." (Colossians 1:10) If you are a fellow believer in Christ, may these devotionals help you increase your knowledge of our Lord and walk worthy of Him. If you do not know Jesus as your personal Savior, may these devotionals convict you of your need for a Savior and persuade you to trust in Him for the free gift of eternal life.

1

New Beginnings

For a righteous man may fall seven times and rise again. (Proverbs 24:16)

* * *

The New Year is traditionally a time of high resolves and emotional commitments. When we turn the calendar page from one year to the next, we naturally think of new beginnings, fresh starts, and a chance to try again. Whatever difficulties and despairs, failures and flaws, that filled the previous twelve months are consciously pushed to the back of our minds as we confidently press forward with private promises to do better.

While such New Year's resolutions are often short-lived, there is an element of biblical truth in the concept of new beginnings. Has it ever occurred to you that God hardwired the potential for new beginnings into the very design of the universe? Think about it. The first person to invent the wheel only discovered what God had already designed, for God created things in circles. The stars and planets are round, they move in orbital cycles. And life, as a result, moves in cycles as well. Every one hundred years, we have a new century. Every 365 days, we have a new year. Every twenty-four hours we have a new day. Every 60 minutes we have a new hour.

There is a good reason for this. We all need the occasional do-over. Indeed, every hero of Scripture needed new beginnings: Adam and Eve after they ate the forbidden fruit; Moses after he killed the Egyptian; David after his adulterous relationship and murderous conspiracy; Elijah after his emotional breakdown in the desert; the disciples after Good Friday; Peter after his shameless denials.

What about you? Do you need a fresh start? The great thing about God's grace is that it never runs out. Though we may fall time after time, God will always be there to welcome us home. Where sin abounds, grace always abounds much more (Romans 5:20). When we are weak, God's strength is always there to lift us up (2 Corinthians 12:9-10).

As you look ahead at the New Year, let me encourage you to do two things. First, make sure you have a relationship with the Lord. This can only come by faith alone in Christ alone, who died and rose again for your sins. If you have never received Christ as your Savior, now is the time to settle this issue once and for all. "Today is the day of salvation." (2 Corinthians 6:2) Don't wait. We are not promised another tomorrow.

Second, if you have already trusted Christ for salvation, let me remind you that God is a God of second chances. Rest in His grace and allow Him to encourage you and guide you throughout the coming year. Jesus said, "Take My yoke upon you and learn from Me, for I am gentle and lowly in heart, and you will find rest for your souls. For My yoke is easy and My burden is light." (Matthew 11:29–30) Happy New Year!

2

Never Look Back?

Listen to Me, you who follow after righteousness, you who seek the Lord: Look to the rock from which you were hewn, and to the hole of the pit from which you were dug. (Isaiah 51:1)

* * *

Someone has said, "When your past calls, don't answer. It has nothing new to say!" There is a lot of truth in that adage. Indeed, the maxim "never look back" is a frequent refrain of visioneering experts and leadership gurus. "Don't dwell on the past," they insist. "Look to the future," they proclaim, "so that you won't be paralyzed by the past." In some respects, this is not bad advice. After all, the Apostle Paul himself pledged to "forget what is behind" and "press toward what lies ahead." (Philippians 3:12–14) However, is it true that there is *never* a time to reflect on the past? Are we forbidden from ever looking back to seek the counsel of history and experience? According to the Bible, there are in fact times when examining events from days gone by can help us learn certain lessons that life has for us to learn.

The prophet Isaiah, for example, encouraged the people of Judah to "look to the rock from which they were hewn." (Isaiah 51:1) He was writing about seven hundred years before Christ, at a time when a heavy, deep darkness had settled over the nation. The Assyrians had invaded, and the Babylonians were threatening. They needed a light to come. The promise of a global kingdom of peace and justice and righteousness that had been given by God several centuries earlier seemed like a distant dream. All hope appeared lost. Then Isaiah the prophet arrived with a message from Yahweh. It was a message that not only looked forward to a better day, but also looked back with a reminder of God's promise of a Messiah who would come and bring light to a dark and dreary world.

Sometimes we have to look back to gain perspective and to bolster our faith. Our faith, like that of the nation of Judah, is built upon the promises of a trustworthy God, and a survey of history validates His trustworthiness. It is important that we recall the lessons of life before they become tucked away in the folds of history, only to be forgotten. Although time offers no "do-overs," the memories of the past live on and serve a valuable purpose in our lives. There are at least three important reasons to look back.

First, the call to look back is a call to remember God's faithfulness. The "rock" from which Judah was hewn refers to God's unconditional promise through Abraham (Isaiah 51:2) that one day the entire world would be blessed through Israel. Even though the present situation for Judah seemed bleak, a survey of history would remind them that God had been faithful in the past and He will be faithful throughout the future.

Likewise, as we recount God's faithfulness, we are emboldened to face the future undaunted by fears of what may lie ahead.

Second, looking back also provides an opportunity to hear the rebukes of life (Proverbs 15:31). Life can be a great teacher. The nation of Judah had a rich history of national experiences on which they could draw for insight. By recalling past experiences, we too can gain wisdom for handling future circumstances and crises. The phrase "learn from your mistakes" is not some empty axiom; it is a biblical principle! As one sage put it, "Wisdom is metabolized suffering."

Finally, as we look back we also gain an opportunity to pass on our heritage to those who come after us. By reflecting on and recording historical experiences, the leaders in Judah were able to teach younger Jews about God's dealings with His chosen nation over the centuries. Similarly, as we rehearse the events of the past, and reflect on them with our children, it provides a teachable moment to pass on the great narrative of faith. "Look what God has done for us." And, "See how good our God is!" become underlying themes that will help navigate us through the ebb and flow of the future.

Let me encourage you to take a moment to look back. Don't linger there. Don't dwell on the past and allow it to paralyze you. However, do take a moment to reflect on the rock from which you were hewn, and rest in God's faithfulness.

WEEKLY WORDS OF LIFE

3

Things That Matter…Things That Don't

Set your mind on things above, not on things on the earth. (Colossians 3:2)

* * *

Lately I have been thinking about the importance of *perspective*. In many ways, our contentment or pleasure in life comes down to our perspective. If we focus our thoughts and attention on the trials of life—all that is negative, disappointing, frustrating, hurtful, difficult, stressful—we are likely to experience only minimal joy as these negative aspects of life eclipse what is really important. On the other hand, if we focus our thoughts and attention on things that really matter, things of eternal value, we are less likely to let the troubles of life consume us.

It is all about perspective. To a woman, a pearl is a jewel that can be worn on her finger, neck, or ear. To a chemist, a pearl is a mixture of aragonite and calcite. To a poet, it is a "teardrop of the sea." To a biologist, it is simply a secretion inside the shells of certain mollusks. But, to a believer, *a pearl is a marvel of God's creation*.

What do you see when you look at life all around you? The Apostle Paul reminds us that "our citizenship is in heaven," not on earth (Philippians 3:20), and thus we should "set our minds on things above, not on things on the earth" (Colossians 3:2). All that is in the world, both good and bad, is temporary; it will pass away some day. It is not worthy of our obsessive attention. Only when we climb to the heights of heaven in our mind's eye, and view life through the lens of eternity, can we begin to prioritize the stuff life is made of and truly appreciate those things that matter.

Tom Landry was one of the greatest football coaches of all-time. He was known not only for his football expertise, but his godly character as well. On one occasion, when asked why he had been so successful, Landry responded to a crowd of more than two thousand students at Baylor University, "In 1958, I did something everyone who has been successful must do, I determined my priorities for my life—God, family, and then football." (Cited in *Dallas Morning News*, March 2, 1978) Landry "set his mind on things above" first.

What about you? What matters most in your life? Are you able to peel away the distractions of life and get to the heart of the matter? At the Milan Cathedral in Italy there are three inscriptions over three respective doorways. Over the right door is this motto: "All that pleases is but for a moment." Over the left door the inscription reads: "All that troubles is but for a moment." Over the center door there is an important reminder: "Nothing is important save that which is eternal." Get into the Word of God daily where you will discover a timeless treasure trove of things that matter for eternity.

4

Life Is Not a Game of "Go Fish!"

He who is full loathes honey, but to the hungry even what is bitter tastes sweet. (Proverbs 27:7)

* * *

My family loves to play games. Board games, card games, group games—it doesn't matter what kind—if there is competition involved, we love it! Years ago, I recall playing a game of *Go Fish* with my son who was about eight years old at the time. It is quite entertaining to watch a child's mind at work. This particular game of *Go Fish* was especially fun because the cards were not the usual numbered playing cards. Instead, they contained a variety of photos-a bicycle, a rain coat, flowers, a lobster, etc. I remember watching my son's wheels turn as he drew cards and narrowed down the possibilities.

"Do you have any c-l-o-w-n-s?" he asked, emphasizing the key word by saying it slowly. "Go fish," I replied. Then I asked, "Do you have any skateboards?" "Ugh! How did you know?" he moaned. And back and forth we went until one of us (usually him) emptied his hand of all his cards. Such fun! The look on a child's face when he wins is priceless!

It occurs to me that many people go through life as if it were a game of *Go Fish*. They evaluate their lives, try to figure out what is missing, and then fill that void with what appears to correspond to their need at the moment. Lonely? Go fish. (Hand me another drink.) Need self-esteem? Go fish. (Tear others down to hide my own insecurity.) Need a new TV or nicer car? Go fish. (Spend money I don't have.) Looking for meaning or purpose in life? Go fish. (Read another self-help book.)

Yet life is not a game of *Go Fish*. No matter how long you play, no matter how many times you draw, you will never find true contentment drawing from the world's stack of cards. The stack is never ending. There always will be more cards to draw. This is because, as the Bible reminds us, "to the hungry soul every bitter thing seems sweet." (Proverbs 27:7) However, to those who have found true peace with God, even the sweetest honey will have no appeal.

Is it your turn to draw? Let me encourage you to set the cards aside and turn to the Word of God as the only real solution to life's problems. No matter what you are facing, the Bible has the answers. Within its pages we find everything we need for life and godliness. Most importantly, the Bible introduces us to Jesus Christ, the Son of God, who died for our sins and rose again. He is the Way, the Truth, and the Life. In Him is life, and that life is the Light of men. In Him, we can have abundant life.

Have you trusted in Jesus Christ to forgive your sin and give you the free gift of eternal life? If not, the time to do so is now before the game ends and you lose. If you already have a relationship with Christ by faith, let me encourage you to resist the temptation to join that old *Go Fish* game. Instead of reaching for that futile deck of cards, pick up the Bible. It will satisfy your every need.

WEEKLY WORDS OF LIFE

5

The Counsel of God's Word

Your testimonies also are my delight and my counselors. (Psalm 119:24)

* * *

In this era where feelings and emotions reign supreme, we often find ourselves justifying our actions based upon the subjective criteria of experience. Feelings are the standard used to verify everything from theological views to political positions. I recall a discussion in which one of my students was unable to support his theological conclusion from the empirical standard of Scripture so finally, in exasperation, he said, "That's just the way I feel about it!" What this student failed to realize is that our theology is not based upon feelings. If it were, theology would be as unpredictable and inconsistent as our ever-changing emotions. Feelings are a dangerous ground on which to build a belief system. Feelings change. Truth does not. Contrary to the prevailing thought of our day, truth exists, and it is embodied in the Word of God.

God has given us the testimony of His Word to validate or invalidate all truth claims. God's Word is living and energetic and when we read it, it pierces our soul and cuts right through all of the human emotion to the heart of the matter. Hebrews 4:12 reminds us that God's Word is so sharp that it can distinguish spiritual truth from our human feelings even when they are so closely intertwined as to resemble joints and marrow, which are often indistinguishable in the human musculoskeletal system. That is why it is crucial to stay in the Word. Many of the beliefs that we hold may in fact be accurate, but if our conclusions are based upon intellectual reasoning rather than the propositional truth of Scripture, our views are prone to change. When someone comes along with a more attractive argument or a stronger appeal to our emotions, we will change our views.

The ancient sage Agur understood this principle well. He wrote, "Every word of God is flawless. He is a shield to those who put their trust in Him." (Proverbs 30:5) Notice, it is the Word of God that is flawless. Man's reason, by contrast, is imperfect. Like everything else in creation, our mind, will and emotions were corrupted by the fall. When sin entered the world, it not only affected our spiritual lives, creating a need for spiritual redemption, it also affected our physical lives, creating a need for physical redemption as well. One day in heaven, our intellectual capacity to reason will be perfect. At that time, all of the redeemed will possess a kind of perfect wisdom that is unknown this side of glory. However, until then, we must rely on God's Word to confirm or reprove our beliefs, attitudes and actions. When we put our trust in God's Word, it shields us from harm. "Your Word is a lamp to my feet and a light to my path." (Psalm 119:105)

Let me encourage you to become less dependent on feelings and more reliant on the Word of God. After all, where have feelings gotten us? Relationships are struggling, morality is declining, and evil is rampant. "The grass withers, and its flower falls away, but the Word of the Lord endures forever." (Isaiah 40:6-8) To become reliant on the Word of God we must become familiar with it. We must study it and store it up in our hearts so that it is readily available when we need it. When feelings and reason compete for our attention, the Spirit of God within us does battle with those feelings. However, He needs the ammunition of God's Word. The psalmist said, "I have hidden Your word in my heart that I might not sin against You." (Psalm 119:11) Do not leave the Spirit of God without a witness within you. Read the Word! Hide it in your heart. It is the best counselor known to man.

WEEKLY WORDS OF LIFE

6

True Love

This is My commandment, that you love one another as I have loved you. Greater love has no one than this, than to lay down one's life for his friends. (John 15:12–13)

* * *

It is February, and that means that our thoughts turn to love. People are always searching for love, aren't they? But sadly, to borrow the words of country singer Johnny Lee, most people are "Lookin' for love in all the wrong places. Lookin' for love in too many faces. Searchin' their eyes. Lookin' for traces of what they're dreaming of."

When it comes to love, what are you dreaming of? Love is one of those words in the English language that has hundreds of uses. We *love* our husband or wife. We *love* our children. We *love* ice cream. We *love* a movie. But what is *true love* anyway?

When I was a senior in high school, the rock band Foreigner released a song that became a big hit. Their song, like Johnny

Lee's country chart-topper years earlier, represents the heart cry of millions of people in the world. It goes like this:

I want to know what love is. I want you to show me. I want to feel what love is. I know you can show me. In my life there's been heartache and pain. I don't know if I can face it again. Can't stop now, I've traveled so far. To change this lonely life. I gotta take a little time. A little time to think things over. I better read between the lines. I want to know what love is. I want you to show me.

Do you want to know what love *really* is? Let's take a little time to think things over from a biblical perspective. We don't have to read between the lines, because the Bible is very clear when it comes to the true meaning of *love*. Just hours before Jesus Christ was betrayed and arrested in the Garden, He spent some intimate time with His eleven closest friends in an upstairs room in a modest Jerusalem home. In that special moment, He washed their feet, instituted the Lord's Supper, and gave them words of encouragement to help them face what was to come in the days and weeks ahead.

He reminded them that true love is a mandate, not an emotion. He said, "This is My commandment, that you love one another." (John 15:12) Love is command, not a convenience. It is active, not passive. We love others because He first loved us. (1 John 4:19) If Jesus' earthly life shows us anything, it shows us that He was never a "Do as I say, not as I do!" sort of leader. He was not asking the disciples, nor us, to do something that He had not already done. Jesus gave us the model of true love. He challenged us to "love one another *as I have loved you.*" (John 15:12)

And just how did He love us? He showed the measure of His love when He laid down His life for us to pay our personal penalty for sin. He said, "Greater love has no one than this, than to lay down one's life for his friends." (John 15:13) We owed a debt we could never pay because of our sin. That debt is eternal separation from a holy God in a literal place of torment called hell. Jesus Christ took my place, and your place, on the cross and paid that penalty on our behalf, even though He was perfect and sinless. His love is a limitless, unconditional, and sacrificial love, and that is precisely how we are to love others.

So what is the meaning of love, then? The Greek word love is the word *agape*. It means, "unconditional affection for another person characterized by a willing forfeiture of your own rights on the other person's behalf." Jesus exemplified this definition perfectly when He died and rose again for our sins. Do you want to know what love is? You must first receive the free gift of eternal life purchased by the loving sacrifice of our Savior, Jesus Christ. You do this by simple faith. Have you trusted in Jesus to forgive your sin and give you eternal life?

Once you have trusted Christ for salvation, only then can you experience *true love* in this earthly life. Instead of looking to *find* or *receive* true love, you will start giving it to others. True love gives because it has received. Find someone to really love today with true, Christ-like love.

WEEKLY WORDS OF LIFE

7

Turn Down the Volume So You Can Hear!

God is our refuge and strength, a very present help in trouble. …Be still, and know that I am God; I will be exalted among the nations, I will be exalted in the earth! (Psalm 46:1, 10)

* * *

Children can say the funniest things. Several years ago, we took our children to the Houston Livestock Show and Rodeo. By nearly unanimous vote, the favorite event was bull riding. There were only two cowboys who managed to hang on for the entire eight seconds. What fun it was to see the look in the kids' eyes and the expressions on their faces as they watched the events unfold in the arena. For me, it was even more fun listening to their comments.

My oldest son, who was ten years old at the time, is known for his decidedly uninhibited outlook on life and the correspondingly transparent comments such an outlook engenders. If you know anything about being in a large sports arena with 25,000 screaming fans, you know how hard it can be to carry on a conversation—even with a person sitting right next to you. At one point during the rodeo, my son leaned over to me and shouted above the deafening clamor of the crowd, "Dad! All this noise is great. I can burp really loud and nobody can hear me!"

It's true. Sometimes the volume can be too loud to hear. It is counterintuitive, really. We normally think of turning the volume *up* when we can't hear it. However, if it is too loud, it distorts the message and may very well drown out other important information. Not that a burp is particularly important, but you get the idea.

The same is true when it comes to our spiritual lives. Often our focus can be so distracted by the hustle and bustle of life, by the deafening din of everyday activities, that we miss the voice of the Spirit. That was the case with Israel many centuries before Christ. The leaders of Israel were engaged in loud and intense conversations among themselves and with other nations in an effort to defend themselves against enemy attacks. The Lord reminded them through the psalmist that if they would only stop striving, God would be their refuge and strength.

"Be still!" God said, "And know that I am God. I will take care of you. I will be your refuge. I will defend you and exalt My Name above all the earth." The verb "be still" (*rāpâ*) is a Hebrew word that literally means "stop fighting so hard." Do you realize that our well-intentioned efforts to serve the Lord may actually drown out His voice if we are not careful?

Sometimes we need to treat life like a giant railroad crossing: Stop! Look! Listen! Stop striving. Look into His Word. Listen to what He has to say. Has it been a while since you heard the calming voice of the Spirit in your life? Maybe it's time to turn down the volume and tune your heart to His voice—the voice of the Bible. God's Word is rich with comfort, guidance, and answers to all of life's problems.

WEEKLY WORDS OF LIFE

8

Are Monsters Afraid of You?

For God has not given us a spirit of fear. (2 Timothy 1:7)

* * *

One of my all-time favorite children's movies is the Disney/Pixar movie *Monsters, Inc*. Every time we watch it as a family I laugh all the way through it. Similar to the *Toy Story* movies, this movie takes you back to your childhood days and invokes warm memories of what it was like to be a kid.

The premise of *Monsters, Inc.* is cute. The land of monsters derives its energy from the screams of children. Each night monsters jump out of closets in children's bedrooms and capture their screams in a vacuum-like container. Then they bring the screams back to the factory ("Monsters, Inc.") where they are converted into energy to light the city. There's a twist, however. It turns out the monsters are more scared of the kids than the kids are of them! When one of the monsters inadvertently brings a child back with him to the land of monsters, the whole city panics. I will not spoil the ending but suffice it to say that both monsters and kids live happily ever after.

This movie begs the question: How many of our fears are really legitimate? Even adults struggle with fear. We may not fear the boogieman in the closet, but we have our own monsters to worry about. Maybe it is the fear of failure. Or the fear of the future. Or financial fears, health fears, fears related to our children, etc. We need to be reminded, "God has not given us a spirit of fear." (2 Timothy 1:7) Fear is one of the devil's chief weapons. His goal is to keep Christians defeated so that we are unproductive in our Christian lives. The way he keeps us defeated is through such weapons as guilt, doubt, and fear. When we fear, we are in essence saying that we think God is not capable of protecting us or providing for us. Worry is a type of fear, and Pastor Adrian Rogers reminds us, "Worry is a mild form of atheism." Fear ultimately signifies a lack of faith. Doubt and fear are twin evils.

Sometimes I think the devil just sits back and laughs as he watches God's children struggle with fear and doubt. He knows that we have no reason to fear him. We should know it too. We have within us a power that is far greater than any of the devil's powers. "Greater is He who is in us than he who is in the world." (1 John 4:4) In reality the devil should be scared of us, not the other way around!

James tells us that when we resist the devil, he flees from us (James 4:7). Too many Christians spend time fleeing from the devil and his weapons instead of using the resurrection power within us to send him scampering off with his proverbial tail between his legs. Let me encourage you to take the offensive in the battle with your fears. Do not let them control you. Read God's Word daily, particularly the Psalms, and allow the Holy

Spirit to strengthen and nourish your spirit. You will soon be reminded of just how much God loves you and just how secure we are in Christ. Then when those pesky fears crop up in your mind, you will be the one laughing, not the devil.

WEEKLY WORDS OF LIFE

9

Only God Is Great

I am the LORD, that is My name; and My glory I will not give to another, nor My praise to carved images. (Isaiah 42:8)

***

The year was 1715 and Louis XIV of France had died. Louis, who called himself, "The Great," was the monarch who made the infamous statement "I am the State!" His court was the most magnificent in Europe, and his funeral was correspondingly spectacular. His corpse lay in a golden coffin. No expense was spared. To magnify the deceased king's greatness, orders were given that the cathedral should be very dimly lighted, with only one special candle set above his coffin creating a sort of halo affect for the King's body as he lay in state.

Thousands gathered for the service and waited in hushed silence as the Bishop Massilon, presiding over the service, began to speak. To the astonishment of all, he began his funeral message by slowly reaching down, snuffing out the candle, and proclaiming, "Only God is great!" I do not know whether or not Bishop Massilon was a believer. In all likelihood he was not, as the Gospel was usually overshadowed by the state church in those days. However, I do know this: Massilon got it right in this instance. *Only God is great!*

God's glory outshines all others. The word "glory" in Scripture means "beauty, splendor and majesty." The Hebrew word is *kavod,* which literally means "heavy." The Greek equivalent is *doxa*, which among other nuances means "power, greatness, and amazing might." God's glory is how we describe the intrinsic effect of all of His attributes. The greatest expression of God's glory is His eternal Son and our Savior. Jesus Christ is "the brightness of God's glory and the express image of His person." (Hebrew 1:3)

Seven hundred years before Christ, the prophet Isaiah reminded God's people that God will never share His glory with another (Isaiah 42:8). He also recorded the words of the seraphim as they cried out, "Holy, holy, holy is the LORD of hosts; the whole earth is full of His glory!" (Isaiah 6:3)

Have you ever wondered, where has all the glory gone? When I look at the world at large, it does not appear to be very glorious. Yet we can be confident that someday, like never before, God's glory will fill this earth.

> *For thus says the Lord of hosts: "Once more (it is a little while) I will shake heaven and earth, the sea and dry land; and I will shake all nations, and they shall come to the Desire of All Nations, and I will fill this temple with glory," says the Lord of hosts. "The silver is Mine, and the gold is Mine," says the Lord of hosts. "The glory of this latter temple shall be greater than the former," says*

*the Lord of hosts. "And in this place I will give peace,"
says the Lord of hosts. (Haggai 2:6–9)*

What a day that will be! What about you? Is God's glory missing from your life? You do not have to wait until Christ returns to experience the fullness of God's glory. You can experience it right now through a relationship with the King of Glory—Jesus Christ. He died for your sins and rose from the dead. Have you trusted Him, and Him alone, for salvation?

WEEKLY WORDS OF LIFE

10

The Amazing Race

Therefore we also, since we are surrounded by so great a cloud of witnesses, let us lay aside every weight, and the sin which so easily ensnares us, and let us run with endurance the race that is set before us, looking unto Jesus, the author and finisher of our faith, who for the joy that was set before Him endured the cross, despising the shame, and has sat down at the right hand of the throne of God. (Hebrews 12:1–2)

***

It was a bitterly cold, snowy Saturday morning in a little town in New Hampshire. The whole town was gathered, as they did every January at this time, to watch the annual Boys Dog Sled Race. Youngsters from all over the region gathered to participate in the one-mile race. The race was open to any boy who desired to enter and thus the participants included everyone from teenagers with fancy sleds and teams of dogs, to young boys with simple two-railed sleds pulled by the family pet.

At the sound of the gun, the participants took off and in no time at all one particular eight-year-old boy, Davy, was left in the dust by the older and stronger contestants. Nevertheless, Davy shouted words of encouragement to Buster, his golden retriever, and the sleigh plodded on. About midway through the race, a mishap occurred in which two of the lead packs came too close to one another and a dog fight ensued. As each dog team came upon the fight, the teenagers struggled to no avail to keep their dogs from joining the fray. Before long all that was visible from a distance was one massive pile of dogs, sleds, and angry young men.

No one seemed able to navigate around it—except, that is, for Davy and Buster. Remaining focused on the finish line, Buster and his young master steered clear of the mess and became the only ones to finish the race. There is a great lesson here: When trouble arises, stay focused on the goal, and *keep on going*.

There is another race that happens not just once a year, but every day. It is not confined to New Hampshire; it is global. This race is much larger and much more significant. It is an amazing race called the race of life. Participants in this grand race face many obstacles and challenges along the way. The question is how can we navigate the race of life successfully to the finish line? The same way Davy and Buster won their dog sled race: *By keeping our eyes on the goal and staying the course.*

The writer of the Book of Hebrews reminds us to "run with endurance the race that is set before us, looking unto Jesus, the author and finisher of our faith." He was writing to a group of Christians in the late 60's AD who were facing unspeakable persecution under the evil regime of the Roman Emperor Nero.

If they were to handle the tragedies and trials of life, the author reminded them, they must keep their eyes on Christ.

In this amazing race of life, Christ sets the example. He is the One who provides the grace and strength we need to keep going. He modeled it in His own earthly life. Jesus kept His eye on the goal which was to glorify His Father. His race took Him through betrayal, scourging and crucifixion, yet He never wavered. He finished the race.

Like Davy and his dog Buster, we too must keep our eyes fixed on the goal and avoid the distractions of life. This requires endurance—steadfast, consistent, daily endurance. When trouble arises, stay focused on the goal and just *keep on going*! It will be worth it all when we see Jesus.

WEEKLY WORDS OF LIFE

11

What Matters Most

But even if we, or an angel from heaven, preach any other gospel to you than what we have preached to you, let him be accursed. As we have said before, so now I say again, if anyone preaches any other gospel to you than what you have received, let him be accursed. (Galatians 1:8-9)

* * *

Allow me to paint a picture in your mind. It is a bright, sunny day. A gentle breeze is blowing. It's not too hot or too cold- just an overall pleasant day. So, you decide to embark on a joy ride through the countryside and take in the scenery. As you are driving down a country road you come upon a roadside sign that reads, *"Caution! This sign has sharp edges on it. Do not touch the edges of this sign."* Speeding past the sign, you think to yourself, "How odd! Why would someone put a sign like that up on the road? That is really weird. It must be some kind of joke."

Moments later, still querying in your mind about the odd sign, you find the front end of your car barreling over a bridge that has been washed out by a recent rain storm. Your car begins to sink in a muddy creek, and you barely escape with your life. Walking back down the road to seek help, you once again come upon that strange sign. But this time you notice some small print at the very bottom of the sign that you had not noticed as you drove past at 35 MPH. You walk up to the sign and discover that the fine print reads: *By the way, the bridge is out up ahead!*

Can you imagine the indignation you would feel? Someone took the time to manufacture a wonderful, smooth, shiny, reflective sign with good and accurate information about the sign's sharp edges, but they failed to emphasize what mattered most. Talk about burying the lede!

We see a similar problem with Christianity these days. We have forgotten what matters most: *The Gospel.* Or at least we seem to have forgotten. Just take a quick look at the best-selling Christian books. Or listen to the radio programs of leading evangelical personalities. Or visit a few popular churches. You will notice plenty of wonderful, smooth, shiny, reflective information that is in many cases good and accurate, but often what matters most is missing or dead wrong.

The Gospel is foundational to Christianity. There is no more important subject in all of Scripture. Yet in this pluralistic age where we are inclined to draw circles of inclusion rather than lines of distinction, many Christians seem unwilling or unable to critically evaluate the accuracy of the gospel being preached. It is easy to become enamored with evangelical leaders whose teaching on certain subjects is deemed encouraging and beneficial, while winking and nodding at the same teacher's erroneous view of the Gospel.

"He is such a passionate speaker!" But is he correct when it comes to what matters most? "He is an expert on financial issues." But is he correct when it comes to what matters most? "She is a gifted communicator on family matters." But is she correct when it comes to what matters most? "This book on marriage is the best I've ever read!" But is the author correct when it comes to what matters most?

What matters most is the Gospel. It does not matter how committed someone may be to other good issues, if he is wrong on the Gospel, his wisdom and insight are built on a faulty foundation. The Bible says that those who are preaching a false gospel are *anathema* (Galatians 1:8-9). Literally, that word means "worthy of severe judgment." The word does not necessarily imply that the one preaching a false gospel is hell-bound himself, though he could be if he has never believed the pure Gospel. The fact is even believers can come under strict judgment (i.e. *be anathematized*; see 1 Corinthians 16:22). The Bible makes it clear that God is displeased by those who propagate a false Gospel.

Why, then, would we ever want to promote or follow those whom God describes as being anathematized? It is really bizarre when you stop and think about it. "Can you recommend a good book on finances?" "Sure! Try this book by so-and-so. God says the author is worthy of severe judgment, but he has great insights on how to manage your money!"

What matters most is the Gospel. If we forget that simple fact, we are in danger of leading others right off the bridge into muddy creek waters. But not to worry, as they are drowning in sin, at least they will have a great marriage, or their finances will be in order, or they will be living their best life now.

WEEKLY WORDS OF LIFE

12

Cloudy Medicine

For whoever shall keep the whole law, and yet stumble in one point, he is guilty of all. (James 2:10)

* * *

Several years ago, my wife Wendy was dispensing a dropper full of medicine to one of our daughters, who was an infant at the time and had a fever. While mom was administering the medicine, our two-year-old son snatched the medicine bottle and tried to play pharmacist by pouring milk from his sippy cup into the open bottle. Before Wendy could get the bottle away from him a drop or two of milk had escaped from the sippy cup and landed right in the medicine bottle. As Wendy looked discouragingly at the cloudy medicine, she realized the entire bottle had to be thrown away. Even though the bottle contained 99% medicine and less than 1% milk, it was still contaminated and unfit for use.

Grace is a lot like medicine. It must be pure for it to be effectual. Grace tainted with any form of human works, behavior, efforts, requirements, merit, and the like, becomes spoiled. It has been nearly 2,000 years since Jesus died and rose again to pay the penalty for sin and provide eternal salvation to all who will simply receive it by faith. Yet efforts to gain heaven on the merits of one's own righteous acts are still contaminating the pure message of grace everywhere you look. The pride of men and women is so strong that it will not allow them to believe that they can get something as valuable as forgiveness and eternal life for free. This is in spite of the fact that the Apostle Paul and the other early church leaders taught unmistakably that the true gospel message was one of salvation by grace through faith as a free gift from God. Paul wrote, "For the wages of sin is death, but the free gift of God is eternal life in Christ Jesus our Lord." (Romans 6:23)

Elsewhere Paul writes, "I do not set aside the grace of God; for if righteousness comes through the law, then Christ died in vain." (Galatians 2:21) What Paul was saying could not be clearer. The righteousness that God's holiness demands is perfect righteousness. If mankind could gain eternal life by keeping the law, or doing good works, Christ's death was irrelevant. Moreover, anyone who hopes to justify himself before God by keeping the law must be willing to keep all of it. Since this is impossible for fallen man, eternal salvation must come from some other source. There must be some other means by which we can gain perfect righteousness. There is. It's called *grace*.

At first this may sound too good to be true. Yet that is what makes grace so amazing. You cannot earn it. It is free! That is the essence of grace. It is undeserved, unmerited favor. You can keep trying to earn heaven by your own righteous behavior if you want to. However, just remember, righteousness gained by human effort is cloudy medicine. James said, "For whoever shall keep the whole law, and yet stumble in one point, he is guilty of all." (James 2:10) In other words, no matter how much medicine is in the bottle, if you add even one ounce of human effort, it spoils the whole batch. When it comes to keeping the law, close does not count. Close only counts in horseshoes and hand grenades, and eternal salvation is not a game. If you want it, you must simply receive it by faith. It is a gift. It cannot be earned. Have you trusted Christ for salvation?

WEEKLY WORDS OF LIFE

13

Warm on the Inside

Then the servant girl who kept the door said to Peter, "You are not also one of this Man's disciples, are you?" He said, "I am not." And the servants and officers who had made a fire of coals stood there, for it was cold, and they warmed themselves. And Peter stood with them and warmed himself. (John 18:17-18)

* * *

The story of Peter's three denials the night Christ was betrayed is well known. In a tragic moment of weakness, Peter, the most vocal of Jesus' supporters during His earthly ministry, and one of His three closest disciples, denied knowing Christ in His hour of greatest need. Reading the account, one cannot help but feel angry. How could Peter do that to Jesus? Yet we are also filled with anguish for Peter because somewhere in the recesses of our minds we all know we might have done the same thing. Faced with the same level of persecution and ridicule who can say if our flesh would not have gotten the best of us too?

What is interesting about the account of Peter's three denials is that twice the gospel writer points out that Peter was warming himself by a fire. (John 18:18, 25) This is significant because later, after Christ's resurrection, Peter would again be given the opportunity to embrace Christ in the context of a fire of coals. The first time we find Peter standing by a fire, he denies Christ three times. The next time we find Peter standing by a fire, he expresses his love for Christ three times. (John 21:9-19) On the first occasion, Peter was warm on the outside but bitterly cold on the inside. On the second occasion, he was both physically and spiritually warm.

Peter's relationship with Christ began with Christ calling on Peter to "follow Me." (Matthew 4:19) Then after three and a half years of fellowship and ministry their relationship comes full circle with Jesus once again calling on Peter to "follow Me." (John 21:21) Did you catch that? The first and last things Jesus ever said to Peter were, "Follow Me." Undoubtedly, when Peter responded to the call the first time, he had no idea how high the cost of discipleship would be. Only through the ups and downs, failures and victories, of ministry did Peter begin to understand what true discipleship really is.

By the time Peter responded to the call the second time, he knew what it meant to follow Christ to the extreme; and follow Him to the extreme is precisely what he did. For the next 35-40 years, Peter served Christ faithfully. There were many times throughout his ministry to the early church that Peter found himself cold on the outside: facing prison or fleeing from the enemies of Christianity. Yet in the midst of it all surely he was warm on the inside. Ultimately, he was martyred for his faith in Rome. Origen tells us that at Peter's own request, he was crucified upside down during the Neronian persecutions. One can only wonder if Peter was cold as he hung on the cross. Perhaps physically—but spiritually he was as warm as he had ever been.

Recently the temperature where I live dropped well below zero. Waiting for my car heater to warm up, I could not help but think of Peter's experience by the fire. The physical cold I was experiencing prompted me to examine my spiritual temperature. Clearly it was cold on the outside; but was I warm on the inside? I quickly said a prayer and asked the Lord for His grace as I seek to walk closely with Him throughout day. What about you? Are you warm on the inside? The first step in lighting a spiritual fire in your life is to place your faith in Jesus Christ, the Son of God, who died and rose again for your sins. Have you done this? If so, continue to rest in the warmth and peace that comes from knowing Him. If not, why not do so right now?

WEEKLY WORDS OF LIFE

14

Don't Just Do Something, Stand There!

Then He said, "Go out, and stand on the mountain before the LORD." And behold, the LORD passed by, and a great and strong wind tore into the mountains and broke the rocks in pieces before the LORD, but the LORD was not in the wind; and after the wind an earthquake, but the LORD was not in the earthquake; and after the earthquake a fire, but the LORD was not in the fire; and after the fire a still small voice. (1 Kings 19:11–12)

* * *

Henry and Elma had been married for fifty years, and their children decided to throw them a party for their golden wedding anniversary. The guest list included many relatives, friends, and neighbors. When the time came for Henry to stand up and toast his beloved wife of fifty years, he got everyone's attention, turned toward Elma, and said endearingly, "After fifty years, I've found you tried and true." Unfortunately, Elma was a bit hard of hearing and did not understand what her husband had said. "Eh? What did you say?" she replied. So, a little louder, Henry repeated, "After fifty years, I've found you tried and true." Still straining to hear, Elma said, "What's that? What did you say?" On the third attempt, Henry bellowed, "AFTER FIFTY YEARS, I'VE FOUND YOU TRIED AND TRUE!" Elma furrowed her brow and retorted, "Well, let me tell you something mister; after fifty years I'm tired of you too!"

Quite often as our years increase, our hearing becomes somewhat dull. It becomes more and more difficult to hear. Even the words of those we love and cherish can become indiscernible. Unfortunately, the same thing is true spiritually. You may have known the Lord for five years, ten years, twenty years, or even fifty years. Nevertheless, perhaps you find it difficult to hear the voice of the Lord. Maybe your spiritual sense of hearing has become dull.

When is the last time you felt the clear, unmistakable direction of the Lord in your life? How long has it been since the Holy Spirit quickened your heart as you read the Word of God, and you knew, without a doubt, that the Lord was speaking to you? Maybe you have been a Christian so long that tradition and the status quo have dulled your sense of hearing. When the Lord speaks to your heart, you have trouble hearing Him because you are out of practice.

Or, perhaps you think that because you have been serving the Lord so long, you no longer need His input and advice. On the other hand, maybe you are so busy doing things for the Lord that you fail to hear His voice speaking to you over the loud, clamoring acts of your Christian service. As a result, you find yourself missing the presence of the Lord in your life when He gently speaks to your heart.

In 1 Kings 19, the Bible records an amazing encounter between Elijah and God. One of the most famous prophets of Israel, Elijah, had has just confronted the prophets of Baal on Mount Carmel and witnessed an incredible display of God's power. Nevertheless he finds himself running scared shortly thereafter from a wicked lady named Jezebel. You would think if there was one person who could hear the voice of the Lord it would be that great prophet Elijah! However, he was so consumed by the mighty demonstrations and miracles of God that He almost missed the voice of the Lord as he sat quivering in fear in a cave. God finally had to grab hold of him and say, "Elijah! Stop. Slow down. Quit doing things for me and just listen to me. *Don't just do something, stand there!"*

What about you? Have you retreated into a cave of fear? Complacency? Boredom? Business-as-usual? Perhaps it is time to stop for a moment, get alone with the Lord and His Word, and hear what God is trying to tell you. Cry out like David, "Cause me to hear Your lovingkindness in the morning, for in You do I trust; cause me to know the way in which I should walk, for I lift up my soul to You." (Psalm 143:8) Don't just do something, stand there. You might just hear that still, small voice of the Lord.

WEEKLY WORDS OF LIFE

15

Identity Crisis

This I say, therefore, and testify in the Lord, that you should no longer walk as the rest of the Gentiles walk....But you have not so learned Christ, if indeed you have heard Him and have been taught by Him, as the truth is in Jesus: that you put off, concerning your former conduct, the old man which grows corrupt according to the deceitful lusts, and be renewed in the spirit of your mind, and that you put on the new man which was created according to God, in true righteousness and holiness. (Ephesians 4:17-24)

* * *

I came across an interesting story from the days of Alexander the Great and his campaign to conquer the world. As the story goes, Alexander the Great received word that one of his soldiers had been engaging continually in improper behavior that was creating a poor reputation for all of the Greek troops. To make matters worse, the soldier's name was Alexander. The commander summoned this rebellious soldier to confront him about his behavior. When the young man arrived at the tent of Alexander the Great, the commander asked, "What is your name, soldier?" The young man replied, "Alexander, sir." The commander then looked him straight in the eye and said rather forcefully, "Son, either change your behavior or change your name."

The lesson here is obvious. As Christians, we bear the name of Christ. In fact, the word Christian means "Christ-like." When we trusted in Jesus Christ as the only One who can forgive our sin and give us the free gift of eternal life, we were *born again*. We took on a new identity as a child of God. By His grace, we joined the family of God. We are a "new man," to use the words of the Apostle Paul in Ephesians 4 and Colossians 3. Thus, when we sin—that is, when we identify with the "old man" in us instead of the "new man"—we are creating a bad reputation for Christ and other Christians.

But more than that, even if our sinful behavior is hidden or secret, we still bring an offense to our namesake, Jesus Christ. Even if the rest of the world does not see our actions, Christ does. How it must grieve Him sometimes to watch us as we ignore the convicting work of the Holy Spirit in our lives and instead indulge in the temptations of the flesh.

What about you? Who are you identifying with? The old man? The new man? The Christian life ultimately comes down to one or the other. The reason so many Christians struggle to live right is because they have an identity crisis. They are identifying with the wrong man in their minds. It reminds me of the time a woman got on an elevator in a tall New York office building and discovered that the only other individual in the elevator was none other than Robert Redford, the movie star. As the elevator slowly climbed upward, she finally mustered enough courage to ask, "Are you the *real* Robert Redford?" He smiled and said, "Only when I'm alone!"

Who are you when you are alone….when no one is looking? That's your real identity. Let me encourage you to identify with Jesus Christ, who gave His life to save you. If you have trusted in Him and Him alone for salvation, then you wear His name. Wear it well.

WEEKLY WORDS OF LIFE

16

All Is Forgiven

He has delivered us from the power of darkness and conveyed us into the kingdom of the Son of His love, in whom we have redemption through His blood, the forgiveness of sins. (Colossians 1:13-14)

* * *

A story out of the heart of Mexico tells of a broken relationship between a man and his son, Paco. As the story goes, the two had been estranged for more than five years stemming from a bitter argument over money. Paco left home in a fit of rage determined never to speak to his father again. As the years went by the father longed to hear from his son but he received no cards, no calls, no contact whatsoever. Eventually, the father's broken heart and undying love for his son prompted him to do something to find Paco. But what could he do? Their town in central Mexico was huge and it had not taken long for Paco to disappear into the crowd.

Desperate but determined to find his son the father placed

an ad in the city newspaper that read: "PACO. THIS IS YOUR FATHER. ALL IS FORGIVEN. MEET ME IN THE CATHEDRAL AT TOWN SQUARE TOMORROW AT NOON. I LOVE YOU!" The next day, trying not to get his hopes up, Paco's father made his way to the cathedral. Upon his arrival he was amazed to find, in addition to his own son, fourteen other young men named Paco hoping to reconcile with their fathers!

This tale illustrates the longing within men and women everywhere for right relationships. No one likes to be estranged. No one wants to have enemies. It is human nature to desire a reciprocal relationship of peace and love. Indeed, mankind is innately relational. From the moment of his creation Adam sought a "suitable companion" in the Garden. Only in the context of healthy relationships can mankind find real fulfillment. It is true: no man is an island. An ancient Proverb rightly cautions, "A man who isolates himself…wages against all wise judgment." (Proverbs 18:1) It is this longing for right relationships that leads to the need for reconciliation when estrangement occurs.

When it comes to our relationship with the Creator, a great and terrible estrangement has occurred. It is called sin. Because of sin, mankind has been alienated from God. The reciprocal relationship of love and peace that existed between Adam and Eve and their Creator in the Garden was broken when sin entered the equation. Because of one man's sin, all mankind has become tainted (Romans 5:12) so that now, we are all strangers (Ephesians 2:12) and enemies of God (Romans 5:10). We are lost in a sea of depravity, far off from the Father (Ephesians 2:13). The Apostle Paul describes mankind's desperate plight with these ominous words: mankind has "no hope" and is "without God in the world." (Ephesians 2:12)

Fortunately, mankind has a loving Father who took the first step in restoring this broken relationship with His creation. God demonstrated the depths of His love for sinful mankind by sending His own Son to die in our place and pay the penalty for our sin (Romans 5:8). God invites mankind, sinful and rebellious though we may be, to come and be restored in our relationship with Him. This offer of a restored relationship with the Creator is not contingent upon our willingness to live right or obey Him or clean up our act. Being reconciled to God is not about what we do or promise to do. It is not about some pledge of allegiance to God as the master of our lives.

It is about faith, plain and simple. Our heavenly Father sent us a message of reconciliation and hope when He sent His own Son to earth to die in our place at Calvary. "All is forgiven!" he shouted from the top of that hill. "Meet Me at the cross!" The message of hope that rang out across the globe nearly 2,000 years ago still echoes today. All who trust Jesus as their only hope for eternal life can be reconciled to God and make peace with their Creator. "But as many as received Him, to them He gave the right to become children of God, to those who believe in His name." (John 1:12)

Everyone who trusts in Jesus Christ for salvation becomes part of the family of God. We have a common bond: We have all been forgiven. Have you been forgiven? If not trust Christ today. And the next time you find yourself at odds with another believer just remember, we are all in this together. This common bond of forgiveness ties us together and fosters unity in the body. We've all been forgiven. At the cross, we are all on equal footing. Let us "endeavor to keep the unity of the Spirit in the bond of peace." (Ephesians 4:3)

WEEKLY WORDS OF LIFE

17

Reign, Reign, Go Away!

So the great dragon was cast out, that serpent of old, called the Devil and Satan, who deceives the whole world…(Revelation 12:9) And I looked, and behold, a white horse. He who sat on it had a bow; and a crown was given to him, and he went out conquering and to conquer. (Revelation 6:2) Now the Spirit expressly says that in the latter times some will depart from the faith, giving heed to deceiving spirits and doctrines of demons…evil men and imposters will grow worse and worse, deceiving and being deceived. (1 Timothy 4:1; 2 Timothy 3:13)

* * *

When I was about ten years old my family lived in a house on a hill. During the summers, my neighborhood friends and I would play a version of "king of the hill" with the kids from the next block. All in good fun, we would have imaginary battles with our "enemies" from down the hill and try to keep them from overtaking our territory.

If you have ever played king of the hill, you know that the object is for one person, the king, to maintain his position on top of a hill by dominating everyone beneath him. Using whatever means necessary (usually a lot of pushing and shoving), the king rules his territory and squashes any and all dissenters. When it came to our neighborhood, my friends and I reigned supreme, and no one, least of all one of the kids from the next block, was going to topple our regime!

Did you know there is a global game of king of the hill taking place right under our noses? It is a battle that has been raging since the Garden of Eden, and it has shifted into high gear over the last 2,000 years. At its core, it is a spiritual, unseen battle between the forces of good and evil. Yet make no mistake; the manifestations of this battle are very tangible.

Satan and his demonic forces have influenced elite world leaders for centuries in an attempt to achieve global domination. His battle plan is deception—he wants to deceive everyone on earth (Revelation 12:9). His goal is to conquer the world (Revelation 6:2). The Bible reminds us that in the present age, evil men and imposters will grow worse and worse, deceiving and being deceived (2 Timothy 3:13). It has been nearly 2,000 years since that prophecy was written—which means that for 2,000 years evil and deception have been increasing in intensity. For Satan, world domination is far more than a good-natured backyard game. He wants to overthrow the Creator and take His place as the sovereign ruler of the universe.

For a while, it will seem like he is winning the battle. In fact, just prior to the Second Coming of Christ, Satan personally will control a man whom the Bible calls the "beast" or the "antichrist," and through him, will set himself up as the global ruler in a one-world government. At first he will be welcomed by most of the world. People will line up behind the antichrist, wholeheartedly embracing the one-world system. Eventually Satan's reign of terror will be exposed. But sadly, by the time his insidious plan is uncovered it will be too late for many.

Fortunately, his reign will be short-lived. A mere seven years after taking control of the world, the Antichrist will be overthrown when Christ returns to take His rightful place as the Messianic King. No one knows for certain when the curtain will rise on the final stages of Satan's plan for global dominance. However, this much is certain: All around us every day the stage is being set for one world government.

We are being pushed and shoved and oppressed by Satan's co-conspirators among the global elite who sit perched atop the hill. Our individual rights are being stripped away all in the name of global progress. Blinded to reality by Satan's intensifying deception, the average person is oblivious to the battle that is raging. Ignorance brings with it a certain feeling of security; but it is a false security. "None are more hopelessly enslaved than those who falsely believe they are free." (Johann Wolfgang von Goethe, 1809)

By contrast, the reality that comes with a biblical worldview brings peace and confidence because we know that one day the temporary king of the hill will be toppled. Until then we trust steadfastly in the promise of God's Word, and eagerly wait for the return of the true King of Kings. Until then we say, "Reign, reign, go away…come again another day…in true Peace and Righteousness and Justice." (Revelation 19:11-15) Come, Lord Jesus!

WEEKLY WORDS OF LIFE

18

Backseat Driver

 man's heart plans his way, but the LORD directs his steps. (Proverbs 16:9)

* * *

Have you ever had the feeling that you are going the right direction, but you just do not know where you are going to end up? You are not really scared because you are kind of enjoying the scenery along the way, but you just do not have a clear picture of exactly where you are headed.

Several years ago, my wife and I had the pleasure of visiting Cancún, Mexico as part of a Caribbean cruise. While there, we paid a fee to one of those shoreline excursion companies to take us parasailing. Unfortunately, a storm arose, and the parasailing company cancelled the activity. When we went back to the beachside kiosk where we had purchased our tickets to request a refund, we discovered that it was closed for the day. We were told we would have to go to the main office to have our refund issued. However, the office was about ten miles away and we had no transportation.

About that time, a nice young man stepped forward and offered to drive us to the office building. Though he did not say it in so many words, the implication was that he expected a significant tip for his services. Feeling we had no other choice, we hopped into this man's car and off we went. We did not know where in the world we were going. Neither of us speaks Spanish, so any backseat driving we attempted was futile.

There we were, crowded into a small, 1970s-era Toyota, watching the sights and sounds of Cancún zoom by. It was definitely a step of faith. Eventually we pulled to a stop in front of a large office building, as our driver exclaimed, "¡Aquí!" We made our way into the office, received our refund, and returned safely to our cruise ship, but not before paying our opportunistic tour guide his well-earned tip.

Lately, life feels a lot like that exciting Toyota ride in Cancún. Sometimes I feel like I am traveling in the right direction, but I am just not sure exactly where I am headed. "How does this part of the journey fit in to the bigger picture of my life?" I wonder to myself. Many of you may be wondering the same thing. "Where in the world are we headed?" Just hang on. Keep trusting the Driver. One day your car will come to a stop in front of a large building and you will think, "Yeah. This is where I am supposed to be." It takes faith to make it through life because God often calls us to enjoy the ride for a while before it all starts to make sense. And there are no backseat drivers with God.

King Solomon understood this principle. He wrote, "A man's heart plans his way, but the LORD directs his steps." Solomon knew that our hearts may be doubting and fretting over all of the sights and sounds as we travel through life. Yet all the while, the LORD is the one driving the car. He is the one that will work everything in our life together to bring us safely to where He wants us to be. So…make your plans. Enjoy the ride. But just remember, in the end God will determine where you are headed. There is great comfort in knowing that, don't you agree?

WEEKLY WORDS OF LIFE

19

Surviving the Culture of Now

Rest in the Lord, and wait patiently for Him; do not fret because of him who prospers in his way, because of the man who brings wicked schemes to pass. Cease from anger, and forsake wrath; do not fret—it only causes harm. (Psalm 37:7–8)

* * *

You've heard of the tyranny of the urgent? These days an even bigger issue is the tyranny of the *now*. With pervasive connectivity and cloud-based data, it has become almost impossible to unplug and simply *do nothing*. Because of the constant clamor of seemingly inescapable technology, it is easy to become overwhelmed by the pressures and stresses of life. The more demands there are on our attention, the more there is to be stressed about!

This has always been the case. Distractions lead to anxiety. Focus leads to peace. King David certainly knew this. He had plenty to distract Him from his task of leading God's nation.

He faced enemies from within, enemies from without, pressure to provide for his own people, personal demons, and more. There were plenty of things to raise David's blood pressure. In Psalm 37 David reminds us how to survive the distractions of the *now* and replace them with steadfast confidence in the One who transcends time.

The principles in Psalm 37 have never been more timely. How can we overcome the rings, tweets, beeps, buzzes, chimes, vibrations, notifications, alerts, and blinking lights that demand our attention *right now*? To understand David's thoughts in Psalm 37, we need to go back to Psalm 36, which was also written by David. Psalm 36 is a Lament Psalm. It expresses distress or sorrow over some issue and asks for divine help. In Psalm 36, David addresses the wickedness of evil people and pleads with God to intervene. His description of the wicked is apt: "there is no fear of God before his eyes." (Psalm 36:1)

Psalm 37 advances the thought of Psalm 36. Psalm 37 is a Wisdom Psalm. It emphasizes themes like right living and the contrast between the righteous and the wicked. In Psalm 37, David urges the righteous not to let the apparent good fortune of the wicked upset them, but to continue to trust in God's ultimate justice.

In Psalm 37:7, David encourages us to "rest in the Lord." The Hebrew word "rest" (*damam*) means "to be quiet." It is the same word that David uses in Psalm 62:5 when he says, "My soul, *wait silently* for God alone, for my expectation is from Him." It is tough to "wait silently" when our smart phones are constantly demanding our attention *right now*.

Although smart phones appeared on the landscape of human history only recently, the problem of distractions is nothing new. Even the disciples of Jesus, who knew nothing of technology, were prone to miss the voice of the Lord amidst the pressures and diversions of the Greco-Roman culture. On one occasion, God the Father had to literally interrupt Peter while he was talking to get him to listen to Jesus. It's a fascinating scene. Take time to read about it in Matthew 17.

I find it interesting that only twice in the New Testament does God the Father speak directly and audibly from heaven to earth; and both times He says the same thing: "This is my beloved Son in Whom I am well pleased." The second of these two times God adds two additional words: "Hear Him!" (Matthew 17:5) This is because Peter was so busy talking, that he missed the presence of the Lord. Wow! Think of that. God had to literally interrupt the first Church leader in order to get a word in edgewise. (I guess some things never change!)

The rings, tweets, beeps, buzzes, chimes, vibrations, notifications, alerts, and blinking lights that demand our attention *right now* are definitely a distraction. They certainly do not have a calming effect. Indeed, usually they stress us out. So, what's the solution? How can we survive this *culture of now*?

King David was spot on when he said that we need to "wait silently" for the Lord. For David, perhaps that meant setting aside his harp; for Peter it meant holding his tongue; for us, maybe it means turning off our smart phones. When we wait silently for the Lord, it changes our focus. Instead of *looking down* at a small, handheld device, we can *look up* and turn our attention to the Lord. With this new perspective, suddenly, all of our problems begin to look very small.

This is why David goes on to say, "Do not fret." (Psalm 37:7) The word "fret" in Hebrew (*charah*) means "to become hot." It is a figure of speech that describes the process of "growing hot with anger." It is similar to the English idiom we use when we describe anger as "making my blood boil" or "growing hot under the collar." It's true; when we get *angry*, we get *hot*. Our blood pressure goes up. That is why when we want someone to calm down we often say, "simmer down."

Do you want fewer distractions and less stress? Do you want to survive the *tyranny of the now*? Wait silently on the Lord; simmer down; and set your mind on things above by staying in the Word of God.

20

Look for the Light

I have come as a light into the world, that whoever believes in Me should not abide in darkness. (John 12:46)

* * *

These are turbulent times. It seems like the world is getting darker and more confusing with each passing day. The prophet Isaiah ministered to the nation of Judah during a time like this. During his ministry, the Northern Kingdom fell to the Assyrians (722 B.C.) and the Israelites were in danger of being swallowed up by the Gentile nations that surrounded them. This Gentile aggression made it imperative for the Israelites to trust God rather than man. Isaiah spoke directly to the unsettled hearts of the Israelites during this time of transition. He challenged God's people to trust Yahweh, not their own fears.

In Isaiah 59:9-10, Isaiah indicts the people of Israel for their lack of faith. One of the consequences of this unbelief was a feeling of total darkness. He wrote, "Therefore justice is far from us, nor does righteousness overtake us; we look for light, but there is darkness! For brightness, but we walk in blackness! We grope for the wall like the blind, and we grope as if we had no eyes; we stumble at noonday as at twilight; we are as dead men in desolate places."

The Israelites understood God's promises and therefore anticipated glorious blessings on their land and their people. However, their present situation was far from glorious. It was dark and gloomy. Nevertheless, God would not totally abandon His people. Though they "grope as if they had no eyes" and "stumble at noonday as at twilight," God's light one day would fill their hearts. Ultimately, this promise was fulfilled in Jesus Christ, the Light of the world.

As I reflected on Isaiah's metaphor about light and darkness, my thoughts turned to the chaos that has enveloped the world over the past few years. At times it seems as though we are groping in darkness. What in the world is going on? Where is the light in this ever-darkening world?

Thinking about darkness reminded me of an experience I had many years ago at Sea World in San Antonio. My children and I were playing in the water park when I suggested that we try the tunnel slide. What I did not realize, but soon found out, was that the tunnel slide was not just a short tunnel followed by hundreds of feet of the more traditional open water slide. Rather, the entire slide was an enclosed tunnel. And it was *dark*...I mean *pitch black*.

As I slid wildly to the bottom for what seemed like an eternity, I kept repeating the following prayer over and over again in my heart: "Lord, get me to the light! Lord, get me to the Light! Lord, get me to the light!" It was the most exhilarating (that's the macho word for *scary*) ride I had ever endured. The tunnel

I was in kept swirling me around violently. Sometimes I was going backwards; sometimes I was going forwards. But then again, who could tell?! I never knew which way I was going to turn next. Most of the time all I could do was just hold on for dear life. When I finally saw a ray of light up ahead I knew the end of the tunnel was near. At that point my prayer changed to, "Lord, I don't care if I come out feet first or head first, just make sure my swimming trunks stay on!"

Sometimes life can be a pretty wild ride, can't it? Like riding down a tunnel slide we often do not know which way is up and which way is down. When life takes us on one of those rides, all we can do is hold on and look for the light. In times like these we need to turn to God and trust Him. He is faithful. He knows when the tunnel ends. He knows where the light is. Stop groping and stumbling and just rest in Him. It will be okay!

WEEKLY WORDS OF LIFE

21

The Golden Key

So when this corruptible has put on incorruption, and this mortal has put on immortality, then shall be brought to pass the saying that is written: "Death is swallowed up in victory." "O Death, where is your sting? O Hades, where is your victory?" (1 Corinthians 15:54-55)

* * *

Death. The word itself is conclusive, leaving no room for ambiguity. It invokes feelings of finality, termination, the end of the story. Death is a topic of discussion best relegated to the twilight hours of the day, not the sort of subject one discusses over morning coffee. It is perceived most often as an enemy to be avoided, not a friend to be embraced. Like the elephant in the room, death is a realty that is never far away—always lurking just beneath the shadows of the mind's eye—but seldom worthy of direct attention. We are conditioned very early in life that death is to be feared and ignored, not faced head on. Most philosophical worldviews incorporate death as an inevitable and terrifying rite of passage that pursues, and eventually overtakes, every human being.

There is one worldview however that does not fear death: the Biblical Worldview. For the Christian, death has no sting. It is swallowed up in victory because Jesus Christ defeated death, hell, and the grave when He rose from the dead. For the Christian, death becomes the golden key that unlocks the riches of eternity. It brings us face to face with our Savior and with other Christians who have gone before us. At death, our faith becomes sight. Death is precious for those who have a relationship with the Creator through faith in His Son, Jesus Christ. "Precious in the sight of the Lord is the death of His saints." (Psalm 116:15)

Have you ever had to say good-bye to someone you love? It is difficult. Sorrow floods our hearts as we deal with the perception of loss. Yet for believers, we know that the separation is only temporary. We will see our loved ones who know the Lord when He returns for the grand reunion in the sky. This blessed hope tempers the sorrow we feel in times of loss.

Our sorrow is soothed even further by the knowledge that the sufferings, limitations, pains, and burdens of mortal life are gone in an instant for our loved one as mortality puts on immortality, and corruption puts on incorruption. Throughout our mortal lives the body groans, eagerly longing to be clothed in perfection. We never were intended to dwell in our mortal, earthly bodies forever. The body is just a tent—a temporary dwelling place until we receive our glorified bodies in eternity.

For some, the groaning of the body is more acute than others. Physical or mental anguish plagues this earthly life day after day until death—in God's time and in God's way—brings welcome relief. The Apostle Paul, who endured untold tortures and persecutions during his earthly life, reminds us that "the sufferings of this present time are not worthy to be compared with the glory which shall be revealed in us." (Romans 8:18)

Still, it is hard to say good-bye. But Scripture gives us the example of the very Son of God Himself, Jesus Christ, who knows what it is like to have to say good-bye to people you love. On the way to Jerusalem for His impending crucifixion, knowing what was about to happen, Jesus thought about His friends. I can picture Him struggling with how to prepare His disciples for His departure. He must have wondered, "How can I explain this to them so they will understand it?" "How will they handle the pain of My death? How in the world do I say good-bye to My friends?"

Jesus had tried to prepare His friends, His disciples, at various points throughout His three-and-a-half-year ministry. "You know, I am going to be leaving you," He told them once in John 7:33. But they did not seem to catch on. He tried again in John 12:34, "The Light will not be with you much longer." They just looked at Him as if He were speaking in riddles. Finally, just hours before He was betrayed, arrested, tried, and crucified, He said it about as plainly and clearly as He could: "In My Father's house are many mansions...I am going away to prepare a place for you...but do not worry...I will come again...and one day we will be together again." (John 14:1-3)

There are two particularly important lessons we can learn from this. First, saying good-bye is difficult. If it is hard for the Savior, it certainly will not be any easier for us. Our emotions are such that we do not handle good-byes very well. Especially good-byes to someone we love so much. Good-byes make us feel a sense of injustice...unfairness. The world seems out of joint, and it hurts. As Christians, we know that death is not an end, but rather a transition—a transition from the limitations of earth to the endless bounties of heaven. But it still hurts.

And this leads to a second lesson we can learn from our Lord's experience with His friends. The answer to the question, "How do you say good-bye to a friend?" is simply that you cannot; and we were never meant to. Jesus, understanding that His disciples would never fully appreciate the nature of His substitutionary death at Calvary until after the resurrection, said it the only way that made any sense at the time. It was not a good-bye at all. It was a "see you later." "I go to prepare a place for you that where I am you may be also some day." The oft-forgotten reality of life is that there are no good-byes for Christians; only temporary separations. The Apostle Paul said it this way: "To be absent from the body is to be present with the Lord." (2 Corinthians 5:8) A few years later, when contemplating his own mortality near the end of his life, Paul added: "My desire is to depart and be with Christ but I also desire to stay here and dwell with you a little longer. I am torn between the two." (Philippians 1:23)

Yes, death is the golden key that unlocks the riches of eternity. But do not miss this next statement. The only way that the terror of death is tamed is by faith alone in Christ alone. Jesus said, "I am the resurrection and the life. He who believes in Me, though he may die, he shall live." (John 11:25) "For God so loved the world that He gave His only begotten Son, that whoever believes in Him should not perish but have everlasting life." (John 3:16) Have you trusted in Jesus as the only One who can forgive your sin and give you the gift of eternal life?

22

God, Glory, and Sleepy Hollow

Then she named the child Ichabod, saying, "The glory has departed from Israel!" because the ark of God had been captured and because of her father-in-law and her husband. (1 Samuel 4:21)

***

Most of my grade school years were spent in the little western Connecticut down of Danbury. As a child growing up in New England, I remember hearing many anecdotes and traditions from early American history. Stories about Williamsburg, Salem, Mystic Seaport, Plymouth Rock, and other legendary sites captured my attention. One of my favorites, though, was the tale of Sleepy Hollow and the Headless Horseman. The town of Sleepy Hollow, made famous by Washington Irving's 1820 short story *The Legend of Sleepy Hollow*, is about forty miles south of Danbury near Tarrytown, NY along the banks of the Hudson River. Perhaps it was its proximity to my hometown that made the story so riveting to me. Regardless,

The Legend of Sleepy Hollow definitely has everything an eleven-year-old boy could want: murder, mystery, and ghosts.

In the story, Ichabod Crane is a skeptical constable sent out to Sleepy Hollow to investigate a rash of decapitation murders alleged to be the work of a headless horseman. Not being a believer in the supernatural, Crane refuses to accept such a preposterous fable. However, he soon becomes convinced. *The Legend of Sleepy Hollow* is a mesmerizing story that, along with *Rip Van Winkle*, earned Irving a place on the list of America's most famous authors.

Given his skepticism, "Ichabod" is a fitting name for Constable Crane. *Ichabod* is a Hebrew term that first appears in the Bible. It is found in a historical account that, like Irving's fictional classic, is a page-turner. In 1 Samuel, we read that the Philistines slaughtered 30,000 Israeli soldiers at the Battle of Aphek, and in the process captured the sacred Ark of the Covenant. When Eli, Israel's high priest at the time, heard the news about the Ark and that his two sons Hophni and Phinehas had been slain in the battle, he was so upset that he fell out of his seat and died! But it gets worse. Eli's daughter-in-law, Phinehas's wife, was pregnant at the time. When she heard the news about the Ark and the deaths of her husband and father-in-law, she went into labor and died giving birth to a son. Just before she died, she declared the name of her new son to be "Ichabod," meaning "no glory."

For Phinehas' wife, the events of that day were too much to bear. They were beyond belief. She could not fathom how such misfortune could befall one family all at once. In her mind, God was absent, and His glory was gone forever. This was not true, of course. God was still very much in control of the situation and Israel had much better days to come (and still does). However, in the tragedy of the moment, her doubt and disbelief led her to immortalize the occasion with the name *Ichabod*.

Similarly, Constable Crane was having trouble making sense of an otherwise senseless situation. The reports coming out of Sleepy Hollow were beyond belief. Perhaps that is why Irving chose the name *Ichabod* for this character. We do not meet too many *Ichabods*, do we? It is not the most flattering name. It has to be right up there with *Lucifer* and *Jezebel* on the list of least used biblical names. The essence of the name Ichabod implies that there is no God—or at least that He is no longer present with you. In Old Testament times, the Ark of the Covenant represented the very presence of Yahweh. Wherever it went, it was accompanied by a cloud, the Shekinah glory of God. When the Ark was stolen, it signified that God's hand of blessing and protection had been removed from Israel. "The glory had departed from Israel." (1 Samuel 4:21)

Though they may not go by that name, we have all met a few *Ichabods* in our day. Perhaps it is the atheist who, like Crane, refuses to believe in the supernatural. Or the skeptic who doubts there is a God. Or maybe it is a believer who, faced with devastating circumstances that stretch his faith to the limits, throws up his hands and gives up. The truth is, all of us act like Ichabod from time to time. Anytime we choose to go it alone, without acknowledging the presence and hand of God in our lives, we have become an Ichabod.

I find it interesting that Scripture equates *glory* with *God's presence*, especially given the world's view of glory. To the world, glory means attaining fame, fortune, or wealth through one's own personal accomplishments—apart from God. According to worldly philosophy, glory belongs to those who are talented, strong, and rich. There is no room for God in the world's definition of glory; but the reality is there can be no true glory without God.

Without the presence of God in your life, all the glory in the world is just a fading light that will one day be extinguished. Jeremiah the prophet sums it up this way,

> *Thus says the Lord: "Let not the wise man glory in his wisdom, let not the mighty man glory in his might, nor let the rich man glory in his riches; but let him who glories glory in this, that he understands and knows Me, that I am the Lord, exercising lovingkindness, judgment, and righteousness in the earth. For in these I delight," says the Lord. (Jeremiah 9:23–24)*

Or to put it more succinctly, "He who glories, let him glory in the Lord." (1 Corinthians 1:31) *The Legend of Sleepy Hollow* is just a fable, and *Ichabod Crane* is just a fictional character, but the reality of living life for the glory of the moment instead of rooted in God's presence is a danger we all face. Where is your glory today?

23

There Is No Comparison

What is more, I consider everything a loss compared to the surpassing greatness of knowing Christ Jesus my Lord, for whose sake I have lost all things. I consider them rubbish that I may gain Christ. (Philippians 3:8, NIV)

* * *

Recently I came across one of those widely circulated emails that lists all of the things that have changed in the world over the past fifty years, and it got me thinking. One of the blessings of living in this modern age is that we are able to do things today that we simply could not do in centuries gone by. Or even a decade ago. Or in some cases, even a year ago! Everything from airplanes to electricity to penicillin helped revolutionize the world. Add to that technological advancements in computers, smart phones, the Internet, nanotechnology, and more, and there really is *no comparison* between daily life today and life in years gone by.

Speaking of air travel, I have done a hefty amount of flying through the years for ministry engagements. I don't fly much anymore, but I recall in great detail how exciting it always was when I would get upgraded to first class because of my frequent flier status. I remember the first time I found myself enjoying some of the finer luxuries in life, like elbow room, overhead bin space, and a meal that you don't have to eat with your fingers. It was wonderful. As my mind wandered to the less fortunate souls sitting in coach, I thought: Ahhh! By comparison, there really is *no comparison*.

And then there's music. It is hard for younger folks like my children to comprehend what listening to music used to be like. It seems like just yesterday I was singing along to my Dad's old reel-to-reel tapes in the living room of our Connecticut house. I was quite the karaoke star long before karaoke became the rage. I'm too embarrassed to reveal whose music was on that old reel-to-reel tape, but I'll give you a hint: His last name is Manilow and his first name starts with a "B." Have you listened to any reel-to-reel tapes lately? Or even a cassette tape? By comparison with today's digital MP3s, or Pandora, or Spotify, there really is *no comparison*.

However, there is one comparison that transcends all others. It is the comparison between life with Christ and life without Christ. Without Christ, even the most enjoyable moments are devoid of meaning. Without Christ, all the riches in the world can't buy everlasting hope. Without Christ, pain and suffering have no resolution. Without Christ, relationships are superficial and fleeting. Without Christ, every victory is hollow and short-lived. Without Christ, the future is uncertain. Without Christ, all is vanity.

Everything pales in comparison to the greatness of knowing

Jesus Christ, God's Son and our Savior. With Christ, we can rejoice no matter what the circumstance. With Christ, we can see the unseen. With Christ, we can walk through the valley. With Christ, even the worst of times fade beneath the glory of knowing Him. With Christ, all things are possible. With Christ, priorities become clear. With Christ, all of our accomplishments, self-attainments, and reasons to boast become far less important as we realize what really matters most. Life with Christ versus life without Him…by comparison there really is *no comparison*. Do you know Christ? If not, let me urge you to place your faith in Him today, as the only hope for eternal life. He loves you so much that He died and rose again to pay your penalty for sin. Trust Him today for salvation.

WEEKLY WORDS OF LIFE

24

Leggo My Ego!

Let another man praise you, and not your own mouth; a stranger, and not your own lips. (Proverbs 27:2)

* * *

I had the pleasure of speaking at a pastor's conference in Orlando some time ago that was attended by several hundred pastors from around the country, and even a few from around the world. I say *pleasure* because indeed it was edifying and challenging to hear some of the keynote messages that were delivered throughout the week. God truly has blessed the body of Christ with some gifted men of God who proclaim His Word boldly and clearly.

Unfortunately, not everything I experienced at the conference was encouraging. As one of the speakers, I had access to the green room where the principal participants in the conference (speakers, singers, emcees, etc.) gathered throughout the day just prior to their appointed time on stage. I arrived at the green room a few minutes before my scheduled stage time, and after being mic'ed by the audio technician, waited just off the stage for my cue.

At the last minute, the conference director decided to bump my presentation to about an hour later. This did not bother me in the least, as my new slot was at a more strategic time in the conference program. With time to kill, I decided to hang out in the green room and listen to several esteemed evangelical leaders engage in an interesting conversation. As I listened, it occurred to me that there were more egos in the room than at a waffle convention. (I know, I know…the waffle brand is spelled with two "g's." Just go with it.)

If I mentioned the name of some of the men in the discussion, chances are you would recognize them. I watched these men repeatedly try to outdo each other. One talked about how his staff posts his social media messages for him (because such menial tasks are beneath him); another mentioned his fancy phone; another talked about his automated Facebook page; and oh, the name-dropping! You should have heard it!

I must confess, my own ego reared its head a few times and I was tempted to chime in with some horn-tooting myself. Then I thought of how many great men of God have fallen and stumbled throughout the years because of their pride; and I thought to myself, "Leggo my ego!" I prayed, "Lord give me the security and confidence in Christ that allows me to speak humbly and graciously with others and avoid the temptation to build myself up." Proverbs 27:2 is a helpful reminder, "Let another man praise you, and not your own mouth; a stranger, and not your own lips."

25

A Few Good Fools

Let no one deceive himself. If anyone among you seems to be wise in this age, let him become a fool that he may become wise. (1 Corinthians 3:18)

* * *

It is getting harder and harder to find a good fool these days. My ministry travels took me across forty states last year, speaking in more than one hundred events; and rarely did I come across a bona fide fool. I had high expectations at one particular conference in Philadelphia. Several hundred Christians packed into an auditorium on the campus of a conservative Bible college, and I was on the lookout for a few good fools. As I got up to speak, I thought to myself, "Surely this place must be loaded with them." However, if they were there, I could not find them.

Where have all the fools gone? There was a time when churches were chockfull of fools. That is not true anymore. In times past, a quick survey of the cultural landscape would reveal a host of fools who stood out among the crowd. They were unique in their appearance, bold in their beliefs, and persuasive in their influence. Two thousand years ago a band of such fools "turned the world upside down." (Acts 17:6) They were called *Christians*.

Over time these avant-garde fools have become the ensemble of the easily influenced. Rather than resembling a *stew pot* where the Christian component remains distinct from the other ingredients in the kettle, our society has become a *melting pot* of compromise and equivocation where most Christians are unwilling or unable to be different. No longer do we see a noticeable contrast between the attitudes and behaviors of Christ-followers and the worldview of the populace.

It occurs to me that what the world needs most in these troubling times are more fools. The world is filled with people who are "wise in their own eyes" and do not "fear the Lord." (Proverbs. 3:7) They are a dime a dozen. But such worldly wisdom is useless. "The Lord knows the thoughts of the wise, that they are futile." (1 Corinthians 3:20) What is desperately needed are Christians who are willing to be "fools for Christ's sake." (1 Corinthians 4:10)

The world needs more Christians who understand that "the message of the cross is foolishness" to the average person. We need Christians who don't mind the moniker "fool" because they realize that the "foolishness of the message they preach" is precisely what the world needs! The foolishness of the cross is the only hope for a lost and dying world. (1 Corinthians 1:18-20)

Christians who blend in with the world, adopt secular thinking, and seek the approval of the masses, have forgotten that the "wisdom of this world is foolishness with God." (1

Corinthians 3:19) Would you rather be a fool in God's eyes or the world's eyes? The Apostle Paul put it well when he wrote, "If anyone among you seems to be wise in this age, let him become a fool that he may become wise." (1 Corinthians 3:18) Do you want to know what we really need if we are truly going to change the world? *Just a few good fools.*

WEEKLY WORDS OF LIFE

26

The Calcium of the Soul

sound heart is life to the body, but envy is rottenness to the bones. (Proverbs 14:30)

* * *

Like many Proverbs, this one puts forth a contrast. It is an example of contrastive parallelism in Hebrew poetry. In this type of poetry, the first line states a principle and the second line amplifies that principle by stating the opposite. The contrast in Proverbs 14:30 is between a "sound heart" and "envy." According to Solomon, a sound heart brings a certain freshness (translated "life") to the body; whereas envy brings a decaying rottenness. The Hebrew word for "rottenness" (*raqab*) literally means "to decay by worm-eating."

That is precisely what envy does: it eats away at us like a worm. It is easy for us to comprehend the idea of envy. We all understand how envy can gnaw at us from the inside out because we have all experienced it. At times we have all allowed the desire for something we do not have to consume us to the point that it is all we think about. Envy is such a powerful and common problem that it is even included in the Ten Commandments ("Thou shalt not covet."). What is the opposite of envy? According to this Proverb it is "a sound heart."

The Hebrew word "sound" (*marpe*) literally means "health, healing or cure." In Hebrew the word is used concretely to refer to a medicine and abstractly it is used of a cure. In the context of this Proverb it carries the idea of a sound or "whole" mind. That is, a heart that is steadfast and content, cured of any ill or unproductive thoughts, will bring freshness to the body. Do you see the contrast? Envy is a parasite that eats away at you, making you sick and eventually unable to function. Contentment, on the other hand, is a medicine that makes you whole. It energizes and revitalizes the soul. It brings healing when outside forces might otherwise make you sick.

The key to good health, then, lies not in the body at large but in the heart. That is why Solomon reminds us to "guard our heart" (Prov. 4:23) because a "merry heart does good like a medicine." (Prov. 17:22) Contentment is the calcium of the soul. If I may borrow a line from a popular ad campaign: "Contentment—it does a body good!" Are you suffering from a heart that is weakened by envy and discontentment? Perhaps you need a contentment supplement. Get into the Word of God and allow it to nourish and satisfy your soul.

27

Unshakable Faith

***

God is our refuge and strength, a very present help in trouble. Therefore we will not fear, even though the earth be removed, and though the mountains be carried into the midst of the sea; though its waters roar and be troubled, though the mountains shake with its swelling. (Psalm 46:1–3)

***

This beautiful psalm written by the Sons of Korah inspired Martin Luther to write his famous hymn, *A Mighty Fortress is Our God*. The psalm, like Luther's hymn, speaks of God as the Lord of Hosts who protects His people from unexpected trouble. From the psalmist's perspective, the earth beneath our feet does not normally move on its own. Likewise, the mountains do not normally shake, and the oceans are not normally in a state of uncontrollable frenzy. These are unusual circumstances. When unexpected things happen, the Lord will provide refuge, the psalmist says. God is always everywhere present; and He never changes. When everything else seems to be changing, the psalmist was confident that God would be there as a "very present help in trouble."

The shaking ground in this psalm is a figure of speech. It is a metaphor for any unexpected, severe trouble that is beyond our control. The psalmist is trying to think of worst-case scenarios that might challenge our faith. Even in times of unprecedented difficulty, God is still God. Whether we see it coming or not; God does. He is never surprised nor caught off guard. Some 3,000 years after this psalm was written, we still have to deal with unexpected events. Believers in the Lord Jesus Christ all over the world are called upon to put their faith into practice by trusting God to see them through unanticipated crises.

These days, it seems like there are metaphorical earthquakes and tidal waves all around us. One minute we are cruising along through life just fine; the next, everything has changed. When unplanned emergencies arise, we must crank up our faith. Sadly, for many believers this faith has laid dormant for weeks or months. We often don't exercise faith until we have to. When things are fine, we don't need God; but when trouble arises, guess where we turn? Unexpected trials separate mature believers from weaker believers. "If you faint in the day of adversity, your strength is small." (Proverbs 24:10) Difficulties will come. How we respond makes all the difference.

Jesus said, "These things I have spoken to you, that in Me you may have peace. In the world you will have tribulation; but be of good cheer, I have overcome the world." (John 16:33) If we hold our heads high and keep marching, in spite of the earth moving beneath us, we are demonstrating the kind of trust that makes us mature and leads us to a deeper relationship with Christ. "My brethren, count it all joy when you fall into various trials, knowing that the testing of your faith produces patience. But let patience have its perfect work, that you may be perfect and complete, lacking nothing." (James 1:2–4)

The Apostle Paul challenged early believers in Thessalonica who were facing persecution and affliction to be encouraged in their faith. He said, "no one should be shaken by these afflictions; for you yourselves know that we are appointed to this." (1 Thessalonians 3:2–3) In other words, God saw it coming and none of their troubles surprised Him. The word "shaken" (*sainō*) in this verse is used only here in the New Testament. Elsewhere in Greek literature it is used to refer to a dog wagging its tail. The idea is that we should not waver back and forth in our faith when we face persecution.

The writer of Hebrews compares our shakable world to the unshakable coming kingdom of God. Since our God is unshakable, our service to Him should not waver in times of trouble. The Bible says, "Therefore, since we are receiving a kingdom which cannot be shaken, let us have grace, by which we may serve God acceptably with reverence and godly fear." (Hebrews 12:28) How do we maintain our faith in the Lord in times of trouble? By exercising it! Each day we need to read God's Word and spend time in prayer—both things that express faith in spiritual matters. We need to trust God for the little things in our lives so that when big troubles come, our natural instinct will be to turn it over to Him.

We must resist the tendency to set specific expectations in life. There is a difference between expectations that are man-made and a general expectancy that God is in control. Expectations are specific ideas formed in our minds to which we think life's circumstances must conform. When life does not play along with our plans, we are crushed. Expectancy, on the other hand, is a general understanding that God is God, and He only wants what is best for us. Expectancy trusts that God's purposes will be accomplished each day, even if they are not always accomplished the way we thought they would be. Expectancy means believing that God's plan is always bigger and better than our measly little expectations, so why not just trust Him and watch the miracles unfold? "Now to Him who is able to do exceedingly abundantly above all that we ask or think, according to the power that works in us." (Ephesians 3:20)

If you have never trusted God for what matters most, your eternal salvation, start there. Trust in God's Son, our Savior, who died and rose again to rescue you from the penalty of sin, hell. He is the only One who can forgive your sins and give you the free gift of eternal life. "For God did not send His Son into the world to condemn the world, but that the world through Him might be saved. "He who believes in Him is not condemned; but he who does not believe is condemned already, because he has not believed in the name of the only begotten Son of God." (John 3:17–18)

If you are already a believer in Jesus Christ, let me encourage you to give up your expectations and embrace a general expectancy that God is in control. He is good. He is faithful. He always has your back. Keep trusting Him.

28

Mending a Broken Heart

The LORD is near to those who have a broken heart, and saves such as have a contrite spirit. (Psalm 34:18)

***

When my oldest daughter was about three-years-old, she used to respond to being scolded by saying, with all of the attendant emotional sobs and tears, "Daddy, you broke my heart!" I can still hear her saying it today. Like most toddlers, she did not like being told, "No!" Her outburst was mostly for dramatic effect. "You broke my heart" was her way of saying that I had hurt her feelings and she was unhappy. She may even have been trying to get me to change my decision. I probably did not help the situation by responding, "Oh, your heart is broken? Bring me my hammer and I'll see if I can fix it!" Some broken hearts go much deeper than a young child's theatrics. Have you ever been brokenhearted?

Have you experienced the deep inner pain that makes you feel like your heart has been ripped from your chest? Heartache so tangible, that it really, truly hurts—physically? Maybe it was caused by the end of a relationship; or perhaps it was the loss of a loved one. Maybe a friend said something or did something that hurt you deeply. We have all been there. Our hearts are tender, fragile organs, both physically and emotionally. The heart represents the seat of our thoughts, feelings and emotions. The heart is where we wrestle with spiritual issues and struggle against sin. The heart is where we contemplate life and form ideas that eventually become actions. When we are faced with a crisis, tragedy or other painful stimulus, our hearts can be broken.

How do we respond when our heart is broken? Or, as one songwriter put it, "How can I mend this broken heart of mine?" Somewhere, someone suggested that time heals all wounds. Perhaps. But there must be something more palatable to the aching soul than simply waiting. "Hang in there. It will get better with time," sounds so empty and useless when your heart is truly weighted down with pain and sorrow. A better solution is found by transcending the temporal arena of time and space and coming at the problem from a spiritual perspective.

King David reminds us, "The Lord is near to those who have a broken heart, and saves (literally, rescues or delivers) such as have a contrite spirit." (Psalm 34:18) The word "broken" (*shabar*) here comes from Hebrew root word that means, "to destroy, shatter, or crush violently." The word "contrite" (*dakka*) is equally strong. It comes from a Hebrew root word that means, "to crush something until it becomes dust or powder." In other words, when David speaks of a "broken heart" and a "contrite spirit" he is speaking of intense hurt and pain. Nevertheless, in the midst of the pain David confidently remarks that Yahweh, the Lord, is with him and will rescue him.

When you are suffering from a broken heart, the tendency is to feel alone and abandoned. However, as believers in Christ, we can take comfort in knowing that our heavenly Father is with us even in the darkest valley. And the reason He is with us is to deliver us safely to the other side of our heartache. Elsewhere David writes, "Yea, though I walk through the valley of the shadow of death, I will fear no evil; for You are with me; Your rod and Your staff, they comfort me." (Psalm 23:4) The phrase "shadow of death" is literally, "the deep, dark valleys." Are you walking through a valley today? Cry out to the Father and let Him know that your heart is broken. He is there. He will respond. "Weeping may endure for a night, but joy comes in the morning." (Psalm 30:5)

/

29

Lord Please Send More Bears!

Better to meet a bear robbed of her cubs than a fool in his folly. (Proverbs 17:12)

***

Bears are a normal part of life this time of year here in the mountains. They get into our garbage, knock over our bird feeders, and they love to stir up our dog, Juneau. As long as they are just a nuisance, bears can be pretty fun to watch. We have captured several videos of a bear climbing up a tree or bounding away toward the river when we scare it off. Of course, bears can be dangerous as well. Just ask the fifty-six-year-old woman from California who was recently attacked by a black bear. She had to endure ten hours of surgery to her face and head to repair the damage done by the mauling. Doctors say she is lucky to be alive.

As bad as a bear mauling may sound, there is something worse. According to the Bible, a "fool in his folly" is an even more ferocious foe. Proverbs 17:12 cautions, "Better to meet a bear robbed of her cubs than a fool in his folly." The word picture here is a vivid one. The only thing worse than an unfortunate encounter with a bear is an unfortunate encounter with a bear robbed of her cubs; and the only thing worse than an unfortunate encounter with a bear robbed of her cubs is an unfortunate encounter with a fool in his folly.

In the book of Proverbs, a "fool" represents the antithesis of God's ways, God's viewpoint. A fool ignores God's perspective and rejects His ideal. A fool is someone who does not behave according to the normal standards of right and wrong or fairness or justice. A fool has his own rulebook. Motivated by pride (the seedbed of all sin), a fool will stop at nothing to achieve his purpose. A fool is obsessed with his agenda and determined to achieve his selfish ends. Like a bear whose single-minded purpose it to protect her cubs, a fool at the height of his folly is focused on protecting only one thing: himself.

There are, of course, degrees of foolishness. Not all bears are killers; and not all fools are self-deceived marauders seeking to destroy anyone who gets in their way. Left unchecked, however, foolishness degenerates into the kind of sinful and hateful behavior that will make a bear robbed of her cubs seem like a harmless furry hamster. That is why Proverbs warns: watch out for a fool in his folly!

Just as you cannot talk an attacking bear out of eating you for supper, likewise there is no reasoning with a fool in his folly. No amount of logic or rationality will convince him to correct course. He is a fool. He has abandoned biblical principles (if he ever had them to begin with) and is dead set on advancing his self-serving agenda, whatever it may be.

Fools bring heartache, frustration, and stress. A good

fool can ruin your day. So, what's the remedy for such an encounter? How can you survive when a fool is pestering you? To begin with, never forget the principle of grace. All of us can be foolish at times. Before picking up the pepper spray, remember to look in the mirror. Secondly, focus on the needs of the fool. What is causing him or her to behave this way? Seek to encourage and graciously love them. If the person is not a believer, share the Gospel! God may use you to help turn a fool into a follower of Christ. Through it all, exercise patience. If all else fails, when you encounter a fool in his folly, I suggest a prayer that goes something like this: "Lord, please send more bears!" At least you have a fighting chance against the bear.

WEEKLY WORDS OF LIFE

30

Old Habits Die Hard

Therefore, laying aside all malice, all deceit, hypocrisy, envy, and all evil speaking, as newborn babes, desire the pure milk of the word that you may grow thereby, if indeed you have tasted that the Lord is gracious. (1 Peter 2:1-3)

***

Everybody loves new things. A new car, a new house, new clothes, new friends, new beginnings. In general, new is usually more exciting than old. The same is true of the new life in Christ. Just as a new winter coat is much better than an old, worn out, flimsy jacket; likewise, the Christian life, if lived according to the guidance of God's Word, is much more pleasant and enjoyable than life without Christ. This fact should motivate us to live by the principles of God's Word.

In 1 Peter 2:1-3, the Apostle Peter challenges his Christian readers to endure hardship and persecution and reminds them that the ways of the Lord are far better than the ways of man.

Having just expounded upon the amazing nature of our new birth in Christ (1 Peter 1:22-25), Peter now says in essence, "In light of your new nature, take off the old nature." The phrase "laying aside" (*apotithēmi*) in 1 Peter 2:1 literally means to "take off." It carries the idea of "putting something down so that you no longer hold on to it" or "taking something off so that you are no longer wearing it." Since we have a new spiritual life, with all of its resources and blessings, why would we continue to "wear" our old way of life? Hanging on to old habits only hinders us from experiencing the full blessings that God has for us day-by-day.

After reminding us of what not to do, Peter goes on to tell us what we should be doing. In verse two, Peter says that believers should "desire" the Word of God in order to grow spiritually mature. It is not enough just to cast off our former ways of sin. If we don't replace our old habits with new ones, we will soon find ourselves slipping back into the old ones once again. The word "desire" (*epipotheō*) literally means "to develop a taste for," or "to long for," or "to pursue with a deep love for." The Word of God is not merely a mechanical resource in our lives. Rather, it brings such joy, peace, and direction to our lives that we ought to long for it like cold water on a hot summer day.

This desire for God's Word has to be cultivated. The more we read God's Word, the more we desire it. The more it nourishes us, the more we want its nourishment. That's why Peter challenges us to "develop a taste for the pure milk of the Word." We need to become so in love with God's Word that anything else tastes bitter by comparison.

In verse three, Peter reminds his readers that they have already "tasted" that the Lord is good. The NKJV begins verse three with "if indeed." The original Greek word has the connotation of "since" or "now that." In other words, Christians already know firsthand that the ways of the Lord are good, refreshing ways. They've "tasted" it. The word "tasted" (*geuomai*) literally means "to experience fully." Those who trust Jesus as their personal savior have experienced the amazing goodness of the Lord in His grace. We know what it feels like to be redeemed and to receive the free gift of eternal life by faith. We know that our God is a good God.

The word "gracious" (*chrēstos*) in 1 Peter 2:3 means "virtuous, good, pleasant, kind and benevolent." "Gracious" is a good summary word to encompass all that God is to us. Since the Lord is so gracious, and since we have experienced His graciousness firsthand, we should develop a taste for His Word and set aside any of our old habits that keep us from fully experiencing the joy of the Christian life. It is true: old habits die hard. We should always remember that for Christians, our new habits are so much better than the old ones. Let me encourage you to get into the Word of God today, and stay there.

WEEKLY WORDS OF LIFE

31

Planks, Specks, and Self-Righteous Prigs!

Judge not, that you be not judged. For with what judgment you judge, you will be judged; and with the measure you use, it will be measured back to you. And why do you look at the speck in your brother's eye, but do not consider the plank in your own eye? Or how can you say to your brother, "Let me remove the speck from your eye;" and look, a plank is in your own eye? Hypocrite! First remove the plank from your own eye, and then you will see clearly to remove the speck from your brother's eye. (Matthew 7:1-5)

* * *

Jesus Christ, the Eternal Son of God, came to earth at His incarnation during a time when God's people had drifted about as far away from God as humanly possible. Judaism was rife with compromise, hypocrisy, arrogance and self-righteousness. The Jewish leaders had convinced themselves that they were righteous—at least more righteous than everyone else—and righteous enough in their own eyes to get into the Kingdom. However, as Jesus bluntly points out, in reality they were far from perfect.

In His famous Sermon on the Mount, Jesus points out that the righteousness that heaven demands is a righteousness that exceeds that of the Pharisees and Sadducees (Matthew 5:20). In fact, the standard for entering heaven is perfection. (Matthew 5:48) In an effort to help these blinded Jewish leaders see the error of their thinking, Jesus pointed out that while they are prating around, boasting about how they have never committed any of the "big sins" such as murder or adultery, in reality their attitudes of hatred and lust have broken these very laws. It is what's in your heart that matters, Jesus declared

Perhaps most offensive was the way these self-righteous Jews looked down their noses at those from the lower tiers of the Jewish social strata. They judged others for their more visible "big sins," yet failed to recognize that their own attitudes were just as offensive to God. Jesus reminded them to be careful about pointing out the speck in their neighbor's eye, when in reality there was a great big plank protruding from their own eye.

Evidently, we have learned very little about pride and self-righteousness in the 2,000 years since Jesus confronted the Jewish leaders. Many Christians in our own generation have wrongly concluded, just like the first century Pharisees, that certain "big sins" justify our judgmental attitudes. In particular, sexual sins seem to be in a class by themselves. However, could it be that while we publicly humiliate those who are guilty of the speck of sexual mistakes, we may be ignoring our much greater plank of arrogance and hatefulness?

C. S. Lewis addresses this very issue quite eloquently. In a paragraph from his book *Mere Christianity* he writes:

> *If anyone thinks that Christians regard unchastity as the supreme vice, he is quite wrong. The sins of the flesh are bad, but they are the least bad of all sins. All the worst pleasures are purely spiritual. The pleasure of putting other people in the wrong, of bossing and patronizing and spoiling sport, and backbiting; the pleasures of power, of hatred. For there are two things inside me competing with the human self which I must try to become; they are the animal self, and the diabolical self; and the diabolical self is the worst of the two. That is why a cold, self-righteous prig, who goes regularly to church may be far nearer to hell than a prostitute. But, of course, it's better to be neither.*

That is vintage C. S. Lewis; and it is thoroughly biblical. Let me encourage us all to beware of the planks in our eyes, lest we show ourselves before God to be "self-righteous prigs." We all need forgiveness of sins, which comes only through faith alone in Christ alone. Have you trusted in Jesus Christ to give you the free gift of forgiveness and eternal life?

WEEKLY WORDS OF LIFE

32

Slow Down and Save Time

See then that you walk circumspectly, not as fools but as wise, redeeming the time, because the days are evil. (Ephesians 5:15–16)

* * *

So much of life comes down to perspective. Perspective can mean the difference between joy and despair, between hope and despondency, between contentment and anxiety. It's all about perspective. A canny old farmer was approached by a stranger one day and asked how much he thought his prized Jersey cow was worth. The farmer thought for a moment, looked the stranger over, then asked: "Are you the tax assessor or has she just been killed by your car." Young David understood the importance of perspective. When the soldiers of Israel saw Goliath, they thought to themselves, "He is so big that we can never kill him." When David saw Goliath, he thought to himself, "He is so big that I cannot miss him."

David's encounter with Goliath illustrates one of the biggest advantages that believers have over unbelievers: *perspective*. Those who know the Lord see things through the lens of the Creator's sovereign plan. We have an eternal vantage point. We understand that life is about much more than you can see, or feel, or touch. We know that no matter what the circumstance, someone greater is always at work. Proverbs 28:5 reminds us, "Evil men do not understand justice, but those who seek the Lord understand all." In other words, those who seek the Lord have a greater understanding—a better perspective—than those who do not.

The Apostle Paul puts it this way, "You were once darkness but now you are light in the Lord." (Ephesians 5:8) He goes on to say that because of the new perspective that comes with knowing the Lord, we should "walk as children of the light." Later in the same passage, Paul explains that "walking as children of the light" means walking "circumspectly." (Ephesians 5:13) The word circumspectly comes from a Greek word, *akribōs*, that means "diligently and accurately." If we walk diligently, with the right perspective, we will make wise choices in life. We will see the bigger picture and have a God-centered attitude no matter what life may throw our way.

Having the right perspective allows us to "redeem the time," as Paul says. The word redeem (*exagorazō*) means to rescue from loss. As we look back over the events of each day, one of two things is always true. Either we made good use of our time by maintaining a spiritual perspective, or we wasted our time because we lived for the moment. Wasted time is lost time. You can never regain a minute lost. To "redeem the time" is to live in such a way that our actions have eternal value in the Kingdom of God. Those who walk circumspectly are storing up untold treasures in heaven.

We often hear the phrase "save time" in the context of doing things faster or more efficiently. The reality is the more deliberate and conscientious our actions, the greater the chance that our time will not be wasted, eternally speaking. Maybe a better way to save time would be to approach each day, not with speed, busyness, and efficiency, but with serious contemplation about the eternal value of the choices we make. Slow down and save time, before it gets away from you!

WEEKLY WORDS OF LIFE

33

A Measure of Assurance

And I give them eternal life, and they shall never perish; neither shall anyone snatch them out of My hand. (John 10:28)

* * *

My favorite kind of cookie is *chocolate chip*. There is scarcely anything better than a hot, just-out-of-the-oven, homemade chocolate chip cookie with a cold glass of milk. When I was a teenager, I used to make them myself, using Mom's family recipe. The first time I did, though, turned out to be quite a fiasco. You see, the recipe card was so old and tattered from years of use that some of the instructions were hard to read. In particular, the measurement amounts were difficult to discern. When it came time to add the brown sugar, I thought it said "12 cups," when in reality it said, "1/2 cup." Big difference! A quick consultation with Mom clarified the matter, and needless to say that first batch of cookies was scrapped and the second batch came out much better.

There is a valuable lesson in this humorous experience. If you do not know the precise measurement a recipe calls for, the result can be disastrous. The same can be said of the believer's assurance. A growing number of Bible teachers and theologians today are suggesting that one's assurance of eternal salvation is based upon "some measure" of good works, without specifying precisely how much good works are necessary to assure one that he indeed is saved.

For example, one popular Christian author writes, "There is no doubt that Jesus saw some measure of real, lived-out obedience to the will of God as necessary for final salvation." Notice his reference to "some measure." If the final, determinative factor in our eternal salvation is "some measure of real, lived-out, obedience to the will of God," one understandably might want to know *how much* obedience? Do I need 12 cups of obedience? Or is it only ½ a cup of obedience? What exactly does this author mean by "some measure?" It sounds conspicuously vague. How can I ever know if I have produced a "measure" of good works acceptable enough to get me into heaven?

Another well-known theologian shares this view of salvation. He suggests that for a person to get to heaven he must not only believe the Gospel, but his faith must produce good works. He writes, "True faith is always accompanied by non-saving, but absolutely necessary works….If there are no good works, there is no true faith." It is not unreasonable to ask how good works can be both "non-saving" but "absolutely necessary" at the same time. If good works are absolutely necessary for final salvation, as these authors suggest, then this makes them determinative in our final salvation. However, the Bible tells us, "For by grace you have been saved through faith, and that not of yourselves; it is the gift of God, not of works, lest anyone should boast." (Ephesians 2:8–9)

Neither author provides a quantifiable way to measure how many good works a person must perform in order to be assured that he is saved. They insist that "good works are absolutely necessary" as "proof" that one is a Christian, but they never give the precise measurement for the proof. Contrary to the assertions of these men (and many others), one's assurance of salvation is *not* based upon his good works.

It is "not by works of righteousness which we have done, but according to His mercy that He saved us." (Titus 3:5) My assurance of eternal salvation is based solely upon the promise of Jesus Christ, my Savior, who said, "I give them eternal life, and they shall never perish; neither shall anyone snatch them out of My hand." (John 10:28) If Jesus meant what He said (and He did!), then my salvation is both sure and secure the moment I place my faith in Him, and I need look only to His promise for assurance. If I look at my works as the basis for assurance-trying to discover some ambiguous measure-I will doubt my salvation every day.

However, if I go back to the source of my salvation to clarify the matter-Jesus Christ Himself-there can be no doubt. He said, "I give you eternal life and you will never perish." Even if I stumble; even if I fall sometimes; whether I have ½ a cup of good works or 12 cups of good works, I can be sure that my faith alone in Christ alone, the Son of God who died and rose again for my sins, has secured for me my eternal salvation. "To him who does not work but believes on Him who justifies the ungodly, his faith is accounted for righteousness." (Romans 4:5) We are "justified freely by His Grace." (Romans 3:24)

In the final analysis, if a "measure of good works" was

necessary for eternal salvation, then the best we could ever hope for is a "measure of assurance." For me, that is not enough. I want to have absolute, 100% assurance of my salvation. What about you? Have you trusted in Jesus Christ and Him alone for eternal salvation? If so, then you can be sure you will spend eternity in heaven.

34

Where Do You Live?

Because of these things the wrath of God is coming upon the sons of disobedience, in which you yourselves once walked when you lived in them. (Colossians 3:6-7)

* * *

Over the years, I have lived in eight different states and twenty-five different cities, some of them multiple times. As I think about my experience in each city, I realize that every town has its own unique culture. For instance, in Danbury, Connecticut you would never think of leaving the house in the winter without gloves, hat, and a scarf. In Houston, Texas few people even own winter gloves or scarves. Such cultural distinctions are not limited to the weather. Language, too, is a big part of culture. In the south, people say things like *fixin'* and *y'all*. In the north they say things like *soda pop* and *you's guys*. The point is, where you live affects the way you live. Some differences are subtle. Others are more pronounced. Regardless, your geographic location has a distinguishable impact on your actions.

Similarly, our spiritual lives are affected by where we dwell. If we live in the realm of the flesh, we are prone to sin. If we live in the realm of the Spirit, we are prone to righteousness. In Colossians 3:7, the Apostle Paul cautioned the Colossians against going back to the pattern of sinful behavior in which they once walked when they "lived in them." In other words, before these people became Christians, they lived in an unspiritual state. Living in such a state meant that acting on their evil desires (Colossians 3:5) came naturally for them. Indeed, sin in the life of all non-Christians comes naturally.

However, once you get saved, you take up residence in the spiritual realm. Or, better said, the Holy Spirit takes up residence inside you when you become "born from above." (John 3:3; James 1:17-18) Living in the Spirit means that you are alive spiritually. It is what the Bible calls regeneration. Those who are alive spiritually (i.e. Christians) naturally produce the fruits of the Spirit (Galatians 5:22-23). Or at least they should. The problem is most Christians act like they are still living in the flesh even though they really live in the Spirit.

Paul said, "If we live in the Spirit, let us also walk in the Spirit" (Galatians 5:25). One modern English version puts it this way: "Since we live in the Spirit, let us keep in step with the Spirit." To go back to my earlier analogy, in the South, we might say to a recently transplanted northerner who continues to use the term soda pop, "Since you live in the south, you should talk like a southerner. It is called Coke!" Those who live in the Spirit should conduct themselves in a manner consistent with the fruits of the Spirit.

It is inconsistent and unnatural for a Christian to continue to commit the same sins he committed before he became a Christian. To do so is to place yourself in bondage to the very power of sin from which you were set free. Listen to Paul's words in Romans 6:16-18.

> *Do you not know that to whom you present yourselves slaves to obey, you are that one's slaves whom you obey, whether of sin leading to death, or of obedience leading to righteousness? But God be thanked that though you were slaves of sin, yet you obeyed from the heart that form of doctrine to which you were delivered. And having been set free from sin, you became slaves of righteousness.*

The question each of us must ask ourselves regularly is, "Where do I live?" If we live in the Spirit, let us act like it!

35

Doctrine Is Dead

Take heed to yourself and to the doctrine. Continue in them, for in doing this you will save both yourself and those who hear you. (1 Timothy 4:16)

* * *

This just in from Reuters News Service: *Doctrine died today*. The news of Doctrine's demise, while tragic, was not entirely unanticipated. It had been battling a terminal illness for many years. Doctrine's storied history is well known. From its powerful birth in the Apostolic age; to its rapid rise to a place of centrality in the Christian life during the early centuries of the Church; to its serious injuries and repression throughout the Medieval period; to its incurable diagnosis during the Enlightenment; and finally its death in this present pluralistic age.

For a brief time, hope of Doctrine's recovery re-emerged during the early 20th century, as Inerrantists and Biblicists put forth aggressive treatment programs that appeared to cause

Doctrine's disease to enter remission. Such hopes turned out to be premature, however. With the onset of postmodern thinking, Doctrine suffered a rapid decline and finally breathed its last breath just this morning.

Reaction to this news has been swift and fairly consistent. One leading evangelical leader wrote, "While we are saddened by this news, we are glad to know that Doctrine's suffering is finally over. Now we can get on with more important matters like relationship building and finding purpose in life." Another popular pastor commented,

> *Our hearts go out to all of those who loved Doctrine and stood by it until the bitter end. We pray that they will gain closure and move forward quickly. We invite them to stop living in the past. Come join the rest of us in mainstream evangelical Christianity as we seek to live our best lives now. Help us change the world through love, peace, and goodwill, rather than through the divisiveness of creedalism.*

Not all Christian leaders have been as diplomatic in their comments. One highly influential Christian personality quipped, "It's about time! Doctrine has had a stranglehold on the thoughts and minds of Christians for far too long. Good riddance!"

The general sentiment across Christendom seems to be one of relief. The climate within Christianity has been characterized by a disdain for doctrinal standards for quite some time. Those who draw lines of theological distinction are perceived as unloving, even hateful or mean, while those who draw circles of inclusion are viewed as more progressive, loving and open-minded. Anyone who claims his view is "right" based upon biblical Doctrine is charged with trying to force his view on someone else. Indeed, the labels "right" and "wrong" have been replaced in favor of less dogmatic phrases like "opinion" and "bias."

Those from the "Can't-We-All-Just-Get-Along" political action committee within evangelicalism already have issued a statement celebrating the dawning of a new day:

> *Finally, once and for all, we can put an end to the judgmentalism, hatred, and arrogance of Doctrine's disciples who insist that right belief is important. Such an archaic philosophy has been on life support for many years and we are heartened that we can now move definitively beyond it to happier days of fellowship, joy, affirmation, and acceptance of all people regardless of their particular beliefs.*

One final addendum to this story. An obscure and little-known Christian leader, who goes only by his first name "Paul," has cautioned that such celebratory response to the death of Doctrine is typical of those whose "consciences have been seared with a hot iron" and whose "itching ears" desire to hear only what makes them feel good. He goes on to point out that Doctrine is necessary for proper behavior and that Christians would do well to "hold fast to sound Doctrine for in so doing it will protect and preserve all who follow it."

It remains to be seen what effect the laying to rest of Doctrine will have on Christianity, but if this "Paul" is correct, straws will blow even more erratically as the blustery winds of pluralism pick up.

36

Bright Lights and Other Distractions

discerning man keeps wisdom in view, but a fool's eyes wander to the ends of the earth. (Proverbs 17:24)

* * *

Teaching a teenager how to drive poses a number of challenges. In the first place, many of the skills we use for driving are instinctive or intuitive and come with practice. For example, you cannot teach a first-time driver how to react when an empty bag of feed corn flies out of the back of a pick-up truck in front of you, and blows right into your path obscuring your view for one, short terrifying moment. In the second place, since teenagers already know everything, very little that is said by their driving instructor will be welcomed and embraced. Teaching our children to drive is just another in a long list of the joys of parenting.

Recently, I was giving one of our children some practice time behind the wheel when we approached a turn onto a busy road. As we looked back to our left to check for oncoming traffic, the bright eastern sun blinded us and made it difficult to see if any cars were coming. It didn't help matters that our windows were coated in dust from our gravel driveway, causing the sun to reflect and create a shadow effect, further shielding our view. Eventually, we were able to gain a degree of confidence that it was safe to make the turn, and the experience became a teachable moment about bright lights and other driving distractions.

Life, like driving, comes down to focus. There are many distractions that easily rob our focus and shift our attention away from the things that matter most. Jesus calls such distractions the "cares of this world" that "choke the Word" in our lives and hinder our spiritual growth (Matthew 13:22). It is axiomatic that our focus determines our direction: *You always hit what you are aiming at.* If your eyes shift to the scenery on your left, your hands on the steering wheel will follow and your car inevitably drifts across the yellow stripe and into the oncoming traffic. Any carpenter worth his salt knows that when hammering nails, you focus on the *nail* not your *thumb*. Because *you always hit what you are aiming at.*

Proverbs reminds us that the eyes of a fool wander to the ends of the earth, but a discerning man keeps wisdom in view. Fools lack focus. Those who are wise keep their eyes on the road. Where is your focus? Are you looking intently into God's Word daily, to maintain the proper perspective and worldview? Or are there bright lights and other distractions that have choked the influence of God's Word in your life, and gotten you off course?

The Word of God is a lamp to our feet and a light to our path (Psalm 119:105). Get in the Word and stay there, lest you find yourself blindsided by all of the trash blowing in the wind.

37

Fruit Inspectors

Beware of false prophets, who come to you in sheep's clothing, but inwardly they are ravenous wolves. You will know them by their fruits. (Matthew 7:15-16)

* * *

Many well-meaning but misinformed Bible students use this passage as a license to judge others. These "fruit inspectors" point a finger at the outward behavior of others and quickly draw conclusions about the genuineness of their salvation. Is that really what Jesus is saying in this passage? Let us take a closer look.

The context of the passage makes it clear that Jesus is not suggesting that we judge the genuineness of one's salvation by looking at his outward behavior. In fact, He expressly forbids such judgment earlier in this same chapter (Matthew 7:1). The fruit to which Jesus refers cannot be outward behavior because the outward appearance of these false prophets is actually very normal and appealing. Jesus says that they come looking like sheep on the outside. Do not miss this point: the fruit of the false prophets is not their behavior! That is precisely Jesus' warning. "Watch out! Do not let their behavior fool you. Just because they are doing good works and acting like believers, does not necessarily mean they are."

So, if fruit is not behavior, what is it? In Matthew 12:33 Jesus says, ". . .a tree is known by its fruit." In the very next verse He explains what fruit is: ". . .out of the abundance of the heart the mouth speaks. A good man out of the good treasure of his heart brings forth good things, and an evil man out of the evil treasures brings forth evil things." (Matthew 12:34-35) There you have it! Fruit refers to what we *say*, not what we *do*!

When Jesus says, "You will know them by their fruits" what He means is that false prophets are exposed by what they *say*, not by what they *do*. They may look like sheep, but when you hear them howl it becomes clear that they are actually wolves. This should be obvious from the context of the passage. After all, the passage is about false prophets, and the best way to determine the accuracy of a prophet is by examining what he says.

The Bible never tells us to look at works to determine the genuineness of one's salvation. Our salvation is not based on good works. "For by grace you have been saved through faith, and that not of yourselves; it is the gift of God, not of works, lest anyone should boast." (Ephesians 2:8–9) If we are relying on our behavior to give us assurance of eternal life, we will doubt our salvation every day because we sin every day. Salvation is a free gift obtained simply by faith in Jesus Christ who died in our place at Calvary and rose from the dead. Only by trusting Him for the forgiveness of sins and eternal life can one be saved.

Do not be swayed by well-dressed, articulate "sheep" who are propagating a false gospel of works. The Gospel is good news. Any presentation of the gospel that includes elements of works is not good news; it is bad information.

WEEKLY WORDS OF LIFE

38

Good, Better, Best

But now He has obtained a more excellent ministry, inasmuch as He is also Mediator of a better covenant, which was established on better promises. (Hebrews 8:6)

***

Have you ever noticed how much we are motivated by comparison? Call it "keeping up with the Jones's." We are a society prone to comparison. When we buy a car, we don't just want a *good* car. We want a *better* car than the next guy. When we purchase clothes, we want *better* clothes than our peers. We always are striving for something better. It is not enough to settle for adequate or even good. We want something *better*.

This tendency is not unique to our American culture. Nor is it unique to our generation. Since the creation of time, mankind has been preoccupied with comparison. The Bible calls it coveting. Eve coveted a piece of fruit. Jacob coveted a birthright. Achan coveted wealth. David coveted a woman.

Ananias and Sapphira coveted notoriety. James and John coveted power; and so on. Throughout time, mankind has consistently engaged in the pursuit of something *better*.

Many people go through life jumping from solution to solution trying to find the answer to life's greatest need. Man's greatest need is salvation; and God sent us a Savior to meet that need. There are many good things that can and do distract people in their search for salvation. Living a righteous, moral life is a good thing; but it is not the best. Performing generous acts of benevolence may even be better; but it is not the best. Being involved in church is a good thing; but it is not the best. Sincere religious passion and devotion may be even better; but they're not the best.

When it comes to salvation, only the *best* will do; and the best is Jesus Christ. The writer of Hebrews expresses this truth clearly when he writes that Jesus is better than anything and everything the world has to offer. He is the best. When is good bad? When it is not the *best*.

If you are searching for salvation, maybe it is time you stopped pursuing so many *good* avenues of righteousness and instead trust in the *best* solution of all. Trust Jesus Christ and Him alone for the gift of eternal life. For those who have already received the gift of eternal life, perhaps it is time to stop living life by comparison and start resting in the *best*. If God provides the best, and only, plan of salvation, will He not also provide the best plan for daily living? "He who did not spare His own Son, but delivered Him up for us all, how shall He not with Him also freely give us all things?" (Romans 8:32)

39

Godly Fear

And if you call on the Father, who without partiality judges according to each one's work, conduct yourselves throughout the time of your stay here in fear. (1 Peter 1:17)

* * *

When my children were younger, I often had the privilege of telling them a story before they went to bed. It was always a special time for us. The anticipation in their eyes, as well as their sweet giggling as I began, was delightful. I usually started by asking them what kind of story they wanted. Inevitably they requested a "scary story." They loved to be scared. This is because the scariest moment of the story was also the most exciting moment for them as the "monster" tickled them relentlessly. As they listened to me tell the scary story they anxiously wondered, "When is the tickle monster going to come?" Their fear, then, was really more of an excited anticipation of something imminent rather than a terror of something awful.

Similarly, Christians are to have a godly fear. We are to fear the Lord—not out of terror of something awful. That kind of terror is reserved for those who have not placed their faith solely in Jesus Christ for the forgiveness of sin and eternal life. That kind of fear is reserved for those who will face Him some day at the Great White Throne judgment. Jesus said in Matthew 10:28, "Do not fear those who kill the body but cannot kill the soul. But rather fear Him who is able to destroy both soul and body in hell."

Believers, by contrast, should have a different kind of fear. It is an anticipation of something imminent. It is an exciting expectation of a future event. Peter put it this way in his first epistle "And if you call on the Father, who without partiality judges according to each one's work, conduct yourselves throughout the time of your stay here in fear." (1 Peter 1:17)

Peter wrote those words to a group of believers who were facing persecution. In his epistle, Peter challenges Christians to endure suffering because it identifies them with Christ's suffering, and it also results in the blessing of rewards when they meet Christ face to face. Peter practiced what he preached. Just a few months after penning this epistle he himself was martyred. The early church father Origen tells us that Peter was crucified with his head downward at his own request. Peter knew what it meant to live the Christian life in a continuous state of fear. Not terror, mind you, but reverent fear knowing that he would face the Lord one day to give an account of his life of service. This kind of steadfast expectation motivates us to serve Christ faithfully.

Implicit within Peter's statement, "conduct yourselves throughout the time of your stay here in fear," is an awareness that we are just passing through this life. Peter calls us "sojourners and pilgrims," which begs the question: How are you spending your time here? Is your life characterized by godly fear? During these times when life is uncertain and many churches and Christians are facing persecution, let us look forward to that time when we will see Christ face to face. May we have an excited anticipation of something imminent rather than a terror of something awful.

WEEKLY WORDS OF LIFE

40

Whose Neighbor Are You?

So which of these three do you think was neighbor to him who fell among the thieves? (Luke 10:36)

***

On July 3, 1988, the navy cruiser USS Vincennes shot down an Iranian jetliner with 290 civilians aboard. There were no survivors. It was a tragic mistake. The ship's captain mistakenly thought they were under attack by an F-14 Iranian fighter jet. Following the incident public opinion polls in America showed that most Americans opposed paying compensation to the victim's families. The cruel treatment of American hostages in Iran was still fresh in many minds. However, contrary to public opinion polls President Reagan approved paying compensation. At a news conference, reporters asked the President if such payment would send the wrong signal. In typical Reagan fashion, the President responded with a potent one-liner, "I don't ever find compassion to be a bad precedent."

What signal are you sending? For many people, the principle

of revenge is much simpler and easier to practice. It comes naturally. However, Christ modeled compassion throughout His earthly ministry, including the supreme example of compassion: Calvary. Christ had a deep love for the physical, emotional, and spiritual needs of others regardless of how they treated Him and regardless of their reputation. Christ simply cared about others. The signal He sent was a signal of compassion. Being moved by compassion always sends the right signal.

What signal are you sending as the world looks on and carefully takes note of your behavior? What signal are you sending, Christian? What signal are you sending, parent? In a world plagued by self-centered, uncaring attitudes, a show of compassion goes a long way. In Luke chapter 10, Jesus confronts a well-respected, well-educated man who in many respects was no different than some Christians today. He was familiar with the Bible. He worshipped regularly. He talked a good talk and walked a pretty good walk. However, when it came to having compassion for others he was sending the wrong signal.

The man was a learned Jewish lawyer. He posed the most important question a person can ever ask: What shall I do to inherit eternal life? Jesus answered the question with a question of His own. In essence, Jesus said, "What do you think?" Whereupon the lawyer recites the Great Commandment, "You shall love the Lord your God with all your heart, with all your soul, with all your strength, and with all your mind, and love your neighbor as yourself." Jesus affirms the man's answer and says, "Do this and you will live." What Jesus meant was this: if you can truly say that you have perfectly kept this commandment then you qualify to enter heaven because the standard for entering heaven is perfect righteousness.

The lawyer's next statement indicates that he thought he had the first part of the Great Commandment down pat. He thought he met the standard when it came to loving God. He needed some clarification about the "love your neighbor" part. Luke tells us that the lawyer was "trying to justify himself." To be justified means to be righteous enough to enter heaven. In other words, this lawyer still did not get the point of Jesus' statement "do this and you will live." He was focused on "doing" things that would qualify him for heaven. That is why his original question was "What must I *do* to inherit eternal life?" Since he was under the impression that loving your neighbor and loving God was all it took, and since he felt he already loved God sufficiently, he wanted to know more about the "love your neighbor" requirement. So, he asks, "Who is my neighbor, anyway?"

What an indictment of his self-centered and pompous attitude! God forbid that he should accidentally show compassion or love toward someone who was not his neighbor. His question was really an attempt to define who his neighbor might be. In Jesus' day, as well as today, there was a category of non-neighbor—*untouchables,* if you will—which included those from other racial, ethnic, religious, or socioeconomic groups. The lawyer was seeking approval for this unloving concept. Jesus answers the lawyer's last question by telling the famous parable of the Good Samaritan.

You know the story well, I am sure, but what you may not notice at first pass is that by the end of the story, Jesus had turned the question around on the lawyer. The lawyer had asked, "Who is my neighbor?" Jesus ends up asking, essentially, *"Whose neighbor are you?"* A good neighbor shows compassion to others regardless of the circumstance, situation, inconvenience, and so on. The lawyer was unwilling to be a good neighbor.

We do not know what ultimately happened to the lawyer, but one thing is certain, if he continued to seek justification through his own efforts, he is spending eternity in hell. The only way to be justified is by *faith*. (Romans 5:1) The righteousness that God's righteousness requires is the righteousness that only Christ can give; and He gives it free of charge to all who trust Him in simple faith for it. The question posed to the lawyer is a good question to ask ourselves as we seek to impact those around us with the message of the Gospel. Whose neighbor are you? What signal are you sending? Are you being a compassionate neighbor to those in need?

41

Hope in Exile

Hope deferred makes the heart sick, but when the desire comes, it is a tree of life. (Proverbs 13:12)

* * *

Waiting is no fun. Nobody knows this better than a child. When our oldest daughter was eight, we took her and her younger siblings to a neighbor's swimming pool. As we walked through the gate into the backyard, we instructed the children to wait by the pool until mom and dad had gotten settled in, and we were ready to watch them. Our eight-year-old sat right on the edge of the pool, anxiously swinging her legs, eagerly awaiting the okay to jump in. Even though the delay was no more than five minutes, it seemed like an eternity to her.

"Can we get in now?" She must have asked that question ten times in five minutes. When we finally gave her permission to get into the water, she was beyond excited. It was instant joy! She was splashing and laughing and kicking in utter exhilaration. For the next two hours, it was non-stop fun in the sun for her and her siblings.

In Proverbs 13:12, Solomon talks about "deferred hope." The Hebrew word "deferred" (*mashak*) literally means "to drag along" as in "trailing seed in sowing." When you plant a seed, you hope that eventually it develops into a plant. However, there is a period of waiting. The real joy in gardening is not realized until you see the sprouts begin to poke through the ground.

Sometimes God's harvest in our life is slow in coming; and sometimes this delay can "make the heart sick," as Solomon reminds us. Nevertheless, when the desire is fulfilled it can be as satisfying as fruit from the "tree of life"—a biblical symbol of God's spiritual and physical renewal. The ultimate desire for which we all hunger and thirst is our eternal redemption in heaven (Romans 8:23). Within each day, there are desires—sometimes little, sometimes enormous—that God puts in our heart. We pray, and hope, and dream. Sometimes God gives us the desires of our heart quickly. Other times He delays fulfillment so that when we receive our desire, it makes us all the more glad.

What is it that you are waiting for today? Do you feel like your hope is in exile? Are you sitting on the edge of a blessing, dangling your feet in eager expectation? Hang in there! God has not forgotten you. In His time you will find yourself swimming in waters of joy, and when you do, what a day that will be.

42

One Nation Under God

B lessed is the nation whose God is the Lord. (Psalm 33:12)

* * *

Our nation chooses a new leader every four years; and like many of you, I enjoy watching the news coverage on election night to learn who our next President will be. Sometimes I rejoice at the results; sometimes I cringe. I am always heartened, though, when I recall that whomever our current leader may be, our country was founded upon many biblical principles; and "blessed is the nation whose God is the Lord." (Psalm 33:12)

Even a cursory review of a few historical facts related to the founding of this country shows the unmistakable hand of God on the birth of this nation. While it certainly is true that not all of the founding fathers were Christians; and while there is no doubt there was a nefarious agenda on the part of many individuals who were instrumental in the establishment of our Republic; and while it should be further noted that the founding of this great country occurred within a complex set of geopolitical world events that were by no means universally godly or Christian, there can be no doubt that *the fingerprints of God are all over the place in American history*!

The very words of the Declaration of Independence, "All men are created equal and endowed by their Creator with certain unalienable rights…," demonstrate that the founding fathers believed in a divine Creator. They lived and operated in a world where the Judeo-Christian ethic was a pervasive part of the culture, even among non-Christians. In the 1600-1700s, the biblical worldview was the prevailing lens through which almost everyone saw life. Thus, it is not surprising to review American history and see references to God everywhere.

For example, the cornerstone of the Washington Monument, laid in 1848, contains a copy of the U. S. Constitution, a copy of the Declaration of Independence, and a copy of the Bible. Engraved on the monument are references to God such as, "Search the Scriptures" and "In God we Trust." The U. S. Capitol building, built between 1793-1858, likewise contains the following references to God: "What Hath God Wrought," "America! God Shed His grace on Thee," and "In God We Trust." Stained glass in the U. S. Capitol Building's chapel depicts George Washington praying beneath the phrase "This Nation Under God."

Above the House Chamber's main door are marble silhouettes of history's twenty-three greatest law makers. Moses is in the *center* and is the only silhouette facing *forward*. The Supreme Court building likewise highlights Moses. Above its eastern colonnade are history's major lawmakers. Moses is in the center holding a depiction of the Ten Commandments.

Speaking of the Supreme Court, in 1892 the Supreme Court ruled 9-0 in a case known as *The Church of the Holy Trinity vs. The United States*, that "This is a Christian nation." Justice David Josiah Brewer cited eighty-seven precedents as he wrote the majority opinion (which as mentioned was unanimous). Here is a quote from Justice Brewer:

> This is historically true. From the discovery of this continent to the present hour, there is a single voice making this affirmation...These are not the sayings, declarations, of private persons: they are organic utterances; they speak the voice of the entire people...These and many other matters which might be noticed, add a volume of unofficial declarations to the mass of organic utterances that this is a Christian nation.

Whatever else may have had an influence on the birth of our nation, the *Christian foundation* simply cannot be denied. One thousand years before Christ, and nearly 2,800 years before America declared her independence from Great Britain, King David asked, "If the foundations are destroyed, what can the righteous do?" (Psalm 11:3) King Solomon later proclaimed, "Righteousness exalts a nation, but sin is a reproach to any people." (Proverbs 14:34)

In 1799, Dr. Jedidiah Morse echoed the sentiments of David and Solomon when he warned, "Whenever the pillars of Christianity shall be overthrown, our present republican forms of government...must fall with them." Again and again this principle has proven true in the history of our country. Whenever America has turned its back on God—destroying our foundation—it has resulted in another giant step in the descent toward Gomorrah, to paraphrase Robert Bork's famous suggestion that the United States is rapidly slouching toward Gomorrah.

Sometimes, Bible-believing Christians are faced with two equally distasteful choices on the Presidential ballot. In such situations, many Christians earnestly and passionately proclaim the "lesser of two evils" adage in supporting their favorite party's candidate. As it has often been pointed out, however, a "lesser evil" is still evil. Indeed, given the character and morals of most mainstream candidates in recent years, a better maxim might be the "evil of two lessers." When you step into the voting booth, let me encourage you to vote through the lens of God's Word, rather than a political party. If Christians will do this consistently, we might just find more choices on the ballot.

Regardless of who is in the White House, one thing is certain: God is not the least bit surprised at the outcome of any election. He remains in full control of this nation, and the entire world. He is working out His plan precisely as He desires. We would do well to remember the words of Proverbs 8:15-16, "By me kings reign, and rulers decree justice. By me princes rule, and nobles, all the judges of the earth." Let us put our faith in the Lord, not in a political party, platform, or person. We are, and always have been, one nation under God; and "Blessed is the nation whose God is the Lord." (Psalm 33:12)

43

Things Are Not Always as They Appear

Joseph said to them, "Do not be afraid, for am I in the place of God? But as for you, you meant evil against me; but God meant it for good, in order to bring it about as it is this day, to save many people alive." (Genesis 50:19-20)

* * *

Perhaps you have heard the story about the kindly old gentleman and his dog Sam. Sam was not the most attractive little mutt. In fact, he was rather ugly. Nevertheless, his owner loved him very much—like the son he never had. Every Sunday this little old man would take his beloved dog Sam on a walk in the neighborhood park. One particular Sunday the man sat on a park bench with Sam at his feet, as was his custom midway through their walk, and began eating his sack lunch. Sam and his owner were not bothering anyone. They were minding their own business.

Soon a rebellious-looking young man appeared with his own dog. Both the youngster and his dog had a mean look to them with bulldog type features to their faces. You could tell they were looking for a fight. Before long, the younger man and his bulldog began taunting the little old man and his ugly dog, Sam. "I bet my dog Spike could kill your ugly mongrel," the young man boasted loudly. Then he looked at his dog and said, "Sic 'em Spike!"

The little old man, without flinching, calmly replied, "I wouldn't do that if I were you." Irritated by the old man's passive comment, the bully once again commanded Spike to attack the frail-looking pooch. The old man calmly repeated, "I wouldn't do that if I were you." As Spike lunged toward unsuspecting Sam, a battle ensued in cartoon-like fashion. There was a lot of barking, dust flying, and dogs running in circles. When the dust settled the result was unexpected. Spike lay defeated, bloodied and torn to pieces by the ugly mutt. Humbled by the experience, the young bully looked at the gentle old man and asked, "Mister, what kind of dog is that anyway?" The old codger replied, "Well, before I cut off his tail and painted him yellow, he was an alligator!"

How many times can you remember responding to a crisis, a situation, or some experience in your life only to find out later that things were not at all the way you perceived them to be? Every day we respond to life's circumstances based on how we see them. Those who see life through the lens of a retributive God are in danger of jumping into a dogfight that turns out to be an alligator fight because things are not always as they appear. Those who see life through the lens of a sovereign, gracious God will trust Him even when things do not seem fair from a human perspective.

A review of the story of Joseph in the book of Genesis indicates that he learned that lesson well. Joseph lived by the motto: *Things are not always as they appear.* He understood that regardless of how things looked, God was at work accomplishing his purpose in Joseph's life. Joseph was the eldest son of Jacob and Rachel and Jacob's eleventh son in all. His father loved him more than all of his brothers. This caused his brothers to hate him.

Their jealousy was aggravated by Jacob's overt expression of favoritism in giving Joseph a beautiful, colorful coat. Every time his brothers saw Joseph wearing that coat, they were reminded of his preferred status with their father. Acting out of jealousy and hatred, his brothers, with the exception of Reuben, resolved to kill him. Reuben intervened on Joseph's behalf and persuaded them to cast Joseph into a pit instead. While the brothers were eating, a company of Arabian merchants came on the scene and Joseph was sold to them for twenty shekels of sliver.

This was the first in a series of bad breaks and unfair life circumstances that Joseph would be called upon to endure. In the years to follow he found himself in jail, falsely accused and frequently mistreated. Through it all, however, he kept the right perspective. He knew that something bigger and greater was at work. He knew that things are not always as they appear.

Years later, Joseph found himself in a position of power and authority in Egypt. When his father Jacob died, his brothers feared that Joseph would seize the opportunity to exact revenge on them for their evil deeds; but he did not. His response to his brothers is one of the most surprising statements in the entire Bible. Joseph said, "Do not be afraid, for am I in the place of God? But as for you, you meant evil against me; but God meant it for good, in order to bring it about as it is this day, to save many people alive." Wow! Joseph knew that even though what happened to him was not good or pleasant—and in fact it was extremely painful—it was all part of God's sovereign plan to accomplish a greater purpose.

Can you say that today? If you find yourself struggling with difficult circumstances or life experiences, remember: *Things are not always as they appear.* God is always looking out for your best interest even if you cannot see how. "We know that all things work together for good" when God is in control (Romans 8:28). And He is!

44

Elusive Peace

Therefore, we do not lose heart. Even though our outward man is perishing, yet the inward man is being renewed day by day. For our light affliction, which is but for a moment, is working for us a far more exceeding and eternal weight of glory, while we do not look at the things which are seen, but at the things which are not seen. For the things which are seen are temporary, but the things which are not seen are eternal. (2 Corinthians 4:16-18)

* * *

It has been nearly thirty years since singer/songwriter Billy Sprague, along with Wayne Kirkpatrick, penned the following lyrics:

> *Yo*u've heard the stories. You've read the message in the pages. You consider the crucifixion: Is it fact or fiction for the ages? Did He really appear like they say that He did? Does it conquer the fear? Did He

die so that we could live? You'd like to think that it's true. But you want to hold the intangible. To fashion the darkness into a familiar shape. To see with your eyes. To know in your mind. Oh ye of so little faith. Only the heart can hold the intangible. There is a chamber in the soul of the believer. It holds reason in defiance. The demanding hand of science may not enter. But let's just suppose how it would be to trade all you know for one ounce of true belief. Then you would learn the peace of that place.

These words describe the outlook of many within our society who are desperately longing for peace. Perhaps more than any other time in our nation's history-certainly more than any other time in our generation-people are searching for an inner peace that seems particularly elusive. These unsettling times have exposed a gaping hole within the hearts of many people where peace belongs yet is not found. In an effort to fill that void, people will turn to various alternatives for peace.

Some trust in riches. Others trust in knowledge. Some trust in the government or the military. Still others trust in friends and family. All of these have the potential to fail us at some time or another. There is only one thing that can bring lasting peace and that is a relationship with the Prince of Peace, Jesus Christ.

You cannot buy peace. It cannot be quantified. Peace cannot be wrapped up in a nice, neat package and tucked away in your file cabinet or bank account. In fact, peace cannot even be stored in the recesses of your mind. Peace is intangible; and "only the heart can hold the intangible." Peace belongs in that chamber of the heart that is reserved for just such a resident.

Those who have faith in Jesus Christ as their Savior have filled that chamber with peace. That is why Christians can take heart even though our outward man is perishing, because we know that inwardly we are being renewed by the presence and power of Jesus Christ.

When your heart is filled with the peace of Christ you begin to look beyond what you can see and feel and touch. You begin to focus on the things that are not seen. You realize that what is seen is only temporary, whereas what is not seen is eternal. Faith is "the substance of things hoped for and the evidence of things not seen." (Hebrews 11:1) Faith is what "holds reason in defiance."

Everyone wants peace, especially in times like these. Everyone wants to lay hold of the intangible quality of peace. However, it is simply impossible to do so apart from a relationship with Jesus Christ. Are you searching for peace today? In the words of Kirkpatrick and Sprague, let me encourage you to imagine for a moment what it would be like to "trade all you know for one once of true belief." Let me encourage you to reach out to Jesus Christ the Son of God who died and rose again for your sin. In simple faith, trust Him to forgive you and give you the gift of eternal life. If you will do that you will learn what true peace is really all about. If you have already done that, believer, then rest in his peace.

… WEEKLY WORDS OF LIFE

45

Believe It or Not

Only let your conduct be worthy of the gospel of Christ. (Philippians 1:27)

* * *

Children usually believe whatever you tell them. They can be quite gullible. Moreover, because their faith is so simple and straightforward, they tend to act on what they believe. Adults, by contrast, do not always act in a manner that is consistent with what they believe.

A humorous anecdote illustrates the point. When our oldest daughter was about five or six years old, she was sitting next to her aunt at the dinner table. When it came time for dessert, she suddenly and without explanation got up from where she was sitting and moved three chairs away. When asked about it, she replied (in a tone that implied, "Isn't it obvious?"), "I am eating chocolate cake and I don't want Aunt Rebekah to get sick."

As it turned out, earlier in the day mention had been made

of Aunt Rebekah's chocolate allergy. Apparently our daughter had assumed that this was an airborne allergy and wanted to shield her aunt from the dangerous chocolate cake virus! It was good for a laugh and a precious memory. As I think back on that incident I am struck with a simple truth: our young daughter acted on what she believed.

There is an important lesson here. When you truly believe something, you act on it. She truly believed that since Rebekah was allergic to chocolate, she might be in danger if she was too close to a piece of chocolate cake. So, believing this with all sincerity she took action and moved her cake away from her aunt.

I am amazed at how often *believers* live like they do not really *believe* the gospel. The gospel is literally "good news." The gospel is the reality that Jesus Christ died for our sins so that we might have eternal life if we simply accept it from Him as a gift. That is really great news! It is life changing news. The reality of our salvation ought to have a profound and pronounced impact on the way we live.

The Apostle Paul told the Philippians, "Let your conduct be worthy of the gospel." In other words, live like you truly believe that you have been saved from sin and are a child of the King. You can tell a lot about what a person believes by watching the way they act. When others look at you what message do they get? Do you believe the Gospel, or not?

46

Thankful for the Little Things

Oh, give thanks to the Lord, for He is good! For His mercy endures forever. (Psalm 136:1)

* * *

Years ago, when I was teaching full time at a Bible college, I worked with a man who was very good at praying. That may sound like a strange observation, but it is true. This man knew how to pray and everyone loved to hear him pray in public. His prayers were convicting because he had a way of reminding us about the little things we take for granted. He often would pray, for example, "Thank you Lord for my feet, which I used to walk into this room!" Or, "Thank you Lord for my hands, which I am using to hold this microphone!" Or, "Thank you Lord for my lungs, which I just used to take a breath!"

When is the last time you thanked God for your feet? Or for your lungs? It is easy to thank God for the big things in life; the big answers to prayer; the big blessings; but sometimes I wonder if we take for granted the little things.

One of the things I love about Jewish history is the way the Israelites passed down testimonies of God's faithfulness through oral tradition. They were very intentional about memorizing songs and sayings that were used to teach their children and grandchildren about their past, specifically the many ways in which God had protected and provided for His people generation after generation. Not only was this used as a way to teach younger members of society, but it also served to motivate and encourage everyone, regardless of age, through good times and bad. At their feasts and festivals, they would recite from memory, or sing, various stories as a reminder of God's everyday hand of blessing.

There is one particular collection of hymns that the Israelites would sing at their three yearly feasts: Passover, Pentecost, and Tabernacles. It is known as *The Hallel*. The Hebrew word *Hallel* is a command that means "praise." *The Hallel* is found in Psalms 113-118 and 136. They also used these psalms on other holy days. These songs were composed by an anonymous hymn writer more than 1,000 years before Christ. At Passover, it was customary to sing Psalms 113 and 114 before the meal and Psalms 115–118 after it to celebrate the Exodus. They also sang Psalm 136, known as *The Great Hallel*, at its climax.

Psalm 136 is unique because it repeats the same refrain in each verse. There are twenty-six verses in Psalm 136, and each one repeats the refrain: "For His mercy endures forever." The Israelites probably sang this song sort of like a responsive reading, with the leaders singing the first part of each verse and the people responding with the refrain. The Hebrew word translated "mercy," is *hesed*, meaning "loyalty, faithfulness, or kindness."

With this song the Israelites praised God for His great acts and for His everlasting kindness. *The Great Hallel* reminds us that God is a kind God—only doing what is in our best interest. He never seeks to do us harm or ill. He knows what we need, and like a good, good Father, only gives us what will help us, even if it is sometimes difficult to recognize it in the moment. God's faithful kindness shows up in countless ways in our lives. As the Israelites sang this song, they were reminding themselves about lots of the big ways that God had shown His kindness through the generations, as well as how He shows His kindness every day in the little things. As I review this psalm, I cannot help but wonder, are we taking some of these little things for granted?

This Thanksgiving, thank God for being a kind God; a loving God; a faithful God. Thank Him for being a good, good heavenly Father Who sent His Son to die in your place on the cross, paying your penalty for sin, and providing eternal life for all who place their faith in Him. Yet don't forget to thank God for the little things as well—things like the air we breathe, the sun that shines, the clothes on our backs, and the eyes you just used to read this devotion.

…

WEEKLY WORDS OF LIFE

47

The Insanity of Ingratitude

Make a joyful shout to the LORD, all you lands! Serve the LORD with gladness; Come before His presence with singing. Know that the LORD, He is God; It is He who has made us, and not we ourselves; We are His people and the sheep of His pasture. Enter into His gates with thanksgiving, And into His courts with praise. Be thankful to Him, and bless His name. For the LORD is good; His mercy is everlasting, And His truth endures to all generations. (Psalm 100:1–5)

* * *

Perhaps you have heard the old fable about a day when the sun did not rise. Six o'clock in the morning came and went, yet still there was no sign of dawn. By seven o'clock, darkness remained. At noon, it was as black as midnight. The morning songs of Steller's jays gave way to the hoot of owls and the distant howls of coyotes. Then came the long, dark hours of the afternoon, one after the other, creeping by. Finally, the evening hours arrived, but no one slept that night. Some wept; some prayed; everyone wrung their hands in anguish. After an endless night of terror and agony, confusion, and bewilderment, millions of tired, tear-streaked faces turned tentatively toward the east. When the sky began to grow red and the sun began to rise, shouts of joy filled the morning air. Millions of voices rang out, "Thank you Lord!" because the sun had risen after just one day of darkness.

The lesson of this simple fable is this: *Sometimes the very consistency of God's great blessings seems to dull our sense of gratitude.* We often take for granted the daily dose of God's blessings and care that are ours to enjoy without even asking. The thankfulness that lies dormant in our hearts should rise in expression each and every morning with the dawning of a new day.

In our country, we set aside a special time each year of reflection on the blessings of God. It is a time of thankfulness. It is a time of *Thanksgiving*. That time is upon us and I cannot help but wonder, "How many of us really need a designated day to help spur our hearts on to thankfulness?" If Thanksgiving was not a national holiday, do you suppose there would be some folks who actually go a whole year without pausing to reflect on God's goodness and express their gratitude to Him? The very idea is insane, when you think of all that we have to be thankful for.

The exhortation for God's people to have a thankful heart is pervasive in Scripture. One of the most well-know examples is found in Psalm 100. Psalms 94-100 are a series of anonymous songs that tell of Israel's great God, Yahweh, who reigns in majesty. Psalm 100 is a sort of doxology or climax to this section of hymns. In it, the writer gives us a glimpse at a thankful heart. He uses five particular Hebrew words, one in each verse (three verbs, one noun, and one conjunction), which give us five key elements of gratitude.

In verse one, we learn that a thankful heart is *active*. "Make a joyful shout to the LORD, all you lands!" (Psalm 100:1) The Hebrew verb "shout" (*rua*) means "to raise a shout; give a blast with a horn; shout a war cry; sound a signal for marching; shout in applause or triumph; cry out in distress." All of these are active actions. Thankfulness is not internal. It is external. Thankfulness may be developed in the heart but it overflows into the life and actions. Jesus said, "Out of the overflow of the heart the mouth speaks." (Matthew 12:34) The psalmist places this verb at the very beginning of the verse for emphasis. It is as if he is saying, "Thankfulness begins with a shout. Say it! Don't think it." It's not enough to *feel* grateful. A true thankful heart is *expressive*.

In verse two, we learn that a thankful heart is *attractive*. "Serve the Lord with gladness; Come before His presence with singing." (Psalm 100:2) The Hebrew noun "gladness" (*simchah*) means "joy, gladness, or mirth as displayed in festivities." Jewish festivities were always very visually appealing. They were *attractive*. They were major productions. Gratitude should be something that is attractive to look at. Sometimes when I hear people expressing gratitude, I cannot help but notice that their words do not seem to match their faces. The psalmist says that gratitude should be expressed with "gladness."

In verse three, we learn that a thankful heart is *accepting* of God for who He is. "Know that the Lord, He is God; It is He who has made us, and not we ourselves; We are His people and the sheep of His pasture." (Psalm 100:3) The

Hebrew verb "know" (*yada*) means to "take special note of." To be thankful is to express confidence in God's provision. A thankful heart begins with a proper understanding of who God is and who we are. Thankfulness requires the right perspective. It accepts God's sovereignty. He is the Creator and we are the created. It accepts God's supervision. We are *His* people. He is the superintendent of our lives. Thankfulness accepts God's shepherding. We are *His* sheep. He cares for us like a shepherd cares for his flock.

This attitude of acceptance—deep trust in God and Who He is, no matter what the circumstance—is perhaps best exemplified by the oft-quoted words of Matthew Henry after he had been robbed. Reflecting on the unfortunate experience, Henry stated, "I am thankful that in all my life I have only been robbed once. I am thankful that they took my wallet and did not take my life. I am thankful that although they took my wallet, it wasn't much. I am thankful that it was I who was robbed and not someone else." What a perspective! He was able to find four reasons to be thankful in the midst of being robbed. He accepted God's *sovereignty* and *supervision* and *shepherding* in his life.

In verse four, we learn that a thankful heart is *adoring* of God. "Enter into His gates with thanksgiving, And into His courts with praise. Be thankful to Him, and bless His name." (Psalm 100:4) The Hebrew verb "bless" (*barak*) means "to adore on bended knee." Four times in this verse the Psalmist uses synonyms for adoration: *thanksgiving,*
praise, be thankful, and *bless.* Adoration demands a heavenly perspective. At the time of writing, Jewish worshippers could literally enter the temple, approaching the very presence of God in the Holy Place, to express their adoration. Today, we

do not have to go to a physical place. However, we do need to symbolically enter the presence of God with a pure heart. Adoration demands humility. Implied within the verb "bless" is this idea of bowing down. You do not look *down* to express gratitude. You look *up* with humble adoration.

Finally, in verse five we learn that a thankful heart is *appropriate*. "For the Lord is good; His mercy is everlasting, And His truth endures to all generations." (Psalm 100:5) The Hebrew conjunction "for" (*ki*) is very common in Hebrew writing. It can mean many different things, but in this construction and context it means "because." A display of gratitude is appropriate *because of* three things. Basically the psalmist spends the first four verses using imperative commands to exhort us to thankfulness and then in verse five he reminds us why thankfulness is called for. We always have a reason to be thankful. He lists three here but there are many. Gratitude is a natural response to God's goodness, grace, and genuineness. God can be trusted—what a blessing!

Gratitude is very appropriate and natural. When we think of all God has done for us, we cannot help but be thankful. To respond otherwise would be insane. Thanksgiving does not require abundance; although most of us certainly fall into that category. It simply requires recognition of what Christ has done for us and then it will flow naturally and appropriately from the heart. "Thanks be to God for His indescribable gift." (2 Corinthians 9:15)

What if Thanksgiving was not a national holiday? Would our hearts still well up in gratitude? Does the sun have to hide for a day for us to realize our blessings? "Enter His courts with thanksgiving," this week. Wherever you are, wherever you go, be thankful.

… WEEKLY WORDS OF LIFE

48

Spiritual Somnambulism

You are all sons of light and sons of the day. We are not of the night nor of darkness. Therefore let us not sleep, as others do, but let us watch and be sober. (1 Thessalonians 5:5-6)

***

Several years ago newspapers recounted the story of a man who fell to his death while sleepwalking. One dark night, he slipped out of a window in his room which was situated at the very top of his house, and while still asleep walked back and forth on the roof for several minutes.

Evidently dreaming of an upcoming party, periodically he would slip back in and then out again of the window, as he was dressing for the occasion. All the while he was singing happy songs. He was careful to preserve his balance upon the roof because his sleep was his security. At one point he walked right over to the edge of the roof and seated himself precariously there. Then, after a moment or two, he retreated and continued preparing for the imaginary party.

Several times he moved away from his dangerous position, but returned to it, always smiling and always sleeping. Suddenly, something caught his eye and awakened him from his stupor. Police theorize it was a light turning on in a window across the street. The eyes of the sleeping man evidently caught it, and, suddenly awakened, he fell to his death with one piercing scream.

This man suffered from *somnambulism*, a condition more commonly known as *sleepwalking*. Although sleepwalking is fairly prevalent, it is rare for it to result in death. Far more dangerous, however, than the average case of sleepwalking is a condition that we might call *spiritual somnambulism*.

Spiritual somnambulism is a raging epidemic that plagues the world today and very few people are aware of it. In fact, that is precisely the reason it is thriving—its victims are oblivious that they are suffering from its effects. What is the primary symptom of this deadly spiritual disease? It is marked by a profound blindness to reality. Those whose minds the god of this age have blinded (2 Corinthians 4:4), walk about always smiling but always asleep to the reality of their spiritual condition. Having never believed the Gospel they are in danger of facing eternity unprepared. They are living "in the dark" and need to be awakened by the light of the Gospel.

The cure is simple: faith alone in Jesus Christ who died and rose again for your sins. The moment you place your faith in Jesus Christ to forgive your sins and give you the free gift of eternal life, you awaken from your sleep and find yourself safe and secure in the arms of Christ. Have you trusted in Jesus Christ alone for eternal salvation?

Yet even after awakening to new life in Christ, believers are not immune to the temporal dangers of spiritual sleepwalking. Satan's deceptive world system makes it very easy to be lulled back to sleep and become blinded to the reality of what is going on around us. That is why Paul reminds us that we are no longer of the night nor of the darkness. Therefore we should not sleep as others do (1 Thessalonians 5:5-6). Having been awakened from our perpetual somnambulistic state, why would we want to return to the very condition from which we have been freed by faith in Christ?

To be sure, even if we "fall asleep" again, we can never lose our eternal salvation. Once we have passed from death to life by believing the Gospel we can never again come under eternal judgment. Jesus made this clear when He said, "Most assuredly, I say to you, he who hears My word and believes in Him who sent Me has everlasting life, and shall not come into judgment, but has passed from death into life." (John 5:24)

There are, nevertheless, consequences for the sleepwalking Christian. When we fall prey to Satan's deceptive world system, when we are taken captive through the empty deceit of the basic principles of this world (Colossians 2:8), we miss out on a host of blessings that God has for His children. More than that, we become pawns in Satan's battle plan. We neutralize our effectiveness in God's spiritual army, and we marginalize ourselves in His Great Commission on earth when we take our eyes off of what matters most.

What are the symptoms of spiritual somnambulism in the life of a Christian? You can spot sleepwalking Christians everywhere. They flit about smiling complacently as they passionately prepare for an imaginary party, never realizing just how precariously close they are to disaster. Their focus, well-intentioned though it may be, is upon things that really don't matter in the big picture. Unwittingly mesmerized by a powerful propaganda machine, most Christians have been lulled to sleep. Like zombies, they go through life unaware and unconcerned with the spiritual realities that are crying out for their attention. They have little or no appetite for Bible study or doctrinal truths. They are content to live life based upon experiential feelings rather than based upon the timeless, infallible, and unambiguous truths of God's Word, the Bible. Like physical somnambulists, *their sleep is their security.*

The remedy? Proverbs 1:22-23 is instructive. "How long, you simple ones, will you love simplicity? For scorners delight in their scorning, and fools hate knowledge. Turn at my rebuke; surely I will pour out my spirit on you; I will make my words known to you." Knowledge unmasks ignorance. Truth exposes a lie. Light nullifies the darkness. Knowledge, truth and light are found only in the Word of God. Since Bible study is a discipline that is noticeably neglected in Christianity today, it is not surprising that so many Christians are asleep. If we want to wake up, we must spend regular time in the Word of God. "We are not of the darkness, so let us not sleep as others do." (1 Thessalonians 5:5-6)

49

A Forever Savior

For there is born to you this day in the city of David a Savior, who is Christ the Lord. (Luke 2:11)

* * *

A former student of mine serves as a pastor in Eastern Europe. Together with his wife and children, he planted a church in one of the most difficult and dangerous mission fields in the world today. He sent me a story about a thirteen-year-old orphan named William who showed up at their church services recently, alone and unannounced. Naturally, the church welcomed and embraced William enthusiastically, and he has been coming to church by himself ever since. He's described as a "respectful, curious, and honest young man."

One Sunday in the middle of my friend's sermon, William raised his hand and asked, "Who is our Savior?" My friend stopped his sermon and looked patiently at young William and replied, "Jesus is our Savior, William. He came to save us—to save us all." Moments later the thirteen-year-old boy raised his hand again. Once again, my friend stopped his sermon and said, "Okay William, one more, go ahead." With the kind of honesty that can only come from an innocent child, William asked, "Will Jesus be our Savior tomorrow too?"

What a great question! Is Jesus still the Savior of the world? A little more than 2,000 years ago, an angel from heaven made an announcement of good news and great joy to a group of Jewish shepherds in a field outside Bethlehem. The angel said to them, "Do not be afraid, for behold, I bring you good tidings of great joy which will be to all people." (Luke 2:10) Then he went on to announce something very significant—something of global importance. He said, "There is born to you this day in the city of David a Savior, who is Christ the Lord." (Luke 2:11) That simple word "Savior" was filled with personal and national significance for these shepherds.

They didn't need to ask, like young William, "Who is our Savior?" Even the most unstudied Jew in that day was familiar with the message of the prophets regarding the Savior. They surely recalled God's words through the great prophet Isaiah when He proclaimed, "I, even I, am the Lord, and besides Me there is no Savior." (Isaiah 43:11) Undoubtedly God's words through the prophet Hosea were well known throughout the land as well, "Yet I am the Lord your God...and you shall know no God but Me; for there is no Savior besides Me." (Hosea 13:4)

We can only imagine how these shepherds must have felt when they witnessed the glory of the Lord in the night sky, and heard this angelic announcement packed with prophetic significance. *The Savior had finally come!* The word "savior" (*sōtēr*) means *deliverer; one who rescues*. For centuries, the world had been looking for the Savior to rescue mankind from the penalty of sin. Now, as promised, at last, He had come. God Himself, through the person and work of His eternal Son, Jesus Christ, had come to earth to rescue mankind. For Jesus, the road to rescue took Him from a lowly manger to a lonely cross, where He died for our sins and rose from the dead. In so doing, He purchased our forgiveness and eternal life.

Jesus offers the gift of eternal life, paid for with His own blood, to anyone and everyone who in simple, childlike faith, will receive it from Him. Like that young orphan, William, many today are asking, "Who is our Savior?" The answer is Jesus. He is the only one who can forgive sin and take away sin's penalty—which is eternal punishment in a literal place called hell.

It has been more than 2,000 years since our Savior came to earth. He is still our Savior today. He will be our Savior tomorrow, and the next day, and the day after that. He is our forever Savior. His payment on our behalf covered the sins of mankind past, present, and future. All those who put their faith in Him can be sure and secure in their salvation for all of eternity. Jesus said, "Most assuredly, I say to you, he who believes in Me has everlasting life." (John 6:47) Have you trusted in Him for the free gift of eternal life?

WEEKLY WORDS OF LIFE

50

God in the Midst

Therefore, the Lord Himself will give you a sign: Behold, the virgin shall conceive and bear a Son, and shall call His name Immanuel. (Isaiah 7:14)

***

In 1989, Sigourney Weaver was nominated for an Academy Award for her leading role in the film *Gorillas in the Mist*, which was nominated for a total of five Oscars. The movie was based upon the life and tragic death of Dian Fossey, and her book by the same title. Fossey's amazing story was also detailed in multiple issues of *National Geographic* magazine.

Dian Fossey was a zoologist and anthropologist who spent more than seventeen years studying mountain gorillas in Africa. In 1967, she established the Karisoke Research Center in the shadows of Mount Bisoke volcano in the Virunga mountain range bordering Rwanda and the Democratic Republic of the Congo. It is reported that locals in the area called her *Nyirmachabelli*—"woman who lives alone in the mountain."

Fossey lived among the rare, gentle mountain gorillas who were threatened by the cruelty of poachers who were tracking them down, one-by-one, and slaughtering them. She began her mission in 1963 on the sides of a 14,000-foot-tall, rain-shrouded volcano, and after several years the gorillas came to accept her as one of their own. Fossey named her gorillas, cradled their babies, and cried with them when they mourned their dead.

She once wrote: "These powerful but shy and gentle animals accepted and responded to my attentions when I acted like a gorilla. So I learned to scratch and groom and beat my chest. I imitated my subjects' vocalizations (hoots, grunts, and belches), munched the foliage they ate, kept low to the ground and deliberate in movement."

After nearly eighteen years with the gorillas, she became like them, dwelt among them, and they were her friends. When faced with danger, she bravely defended them. She was their hero. And on the morning of December 27, 1985, she was knifed and murdered, apparently by poachers whose trade she had sought to destroy. She died for those she came to live among and to save.

Two thousand years ago, Christ left the comforts of His home for the fog-shrouded volcano of earth. He identified with us, learned our names, wept with us. He, too, died for those He came to live among and to save. Jesus once said: "Greater love has no one than this, than to lay down one's life for his friend." (John 15:13)

The story of Dian Fossey was about *gorillas in the mist*. The story of Christ is about *God in the midst*. Eight centuries before Christ, the prophet Isaiah proclaimed that the baby born in Bethlehem would be called, Immanuel—*God with us; a*nd that is precisely what happened 2,000 years ago. God left the eternal realm of glory, came to earth, and put on human flesh to rescue a lost and dying world from the penalty of sin.

Let us never forget that the story of Christmas is a story of unparalleled love and compassion. It is a story of humility, grace, and sacrifice. The essence of the Gospel message is *God in the midst*. God in the midst of sin-stricken, helpless, and hurting people. God in the midst of a world in desperate need of a hero. God in the midst of you and me. Do you know Him?

Jesus Christ, the Son of God, took your place on the cross, died and rose again for your sins. He offers freely to all the gift of forgiveness and eternal life if you will simply trust Him and Him alone for it.

WEEKLY WORDS OF LIFE

51

A Truly White Christmas

Come now, and let us reason together, says the Lord. Though your sins are like scarlet, they shall be as white as snow; though they are red like crimson, they shall be as wool. (Isaiah 1:18)

* * *

Here in the Rocky Mountains, we get more than our share of snow. Indeed, we measure snow in feet not inches. Much of wintertime is spent tuned in to the *Weather Channel* watching the forecast and reading the advisories. Travel through the mountain passes can be treacherous with blizzards, whiteouts, and icy roads. By March we are longing to see more green and less white. In spite of these seasonal hardships, I just cannot seem to shake my romantic relationship with that first snowfall of winter.

There is nothing quite like it. Watching the snowflakes float effortlessly toward the ground. Seeing rooftops and roads slowly turn white. Beholding the tall pines as they become draped in snowy gowns. Something about it seems to fill the air with the aroma of smoke even before the first fireplace lights up.

Then as November gives way to December, and the brown and orange decorations of Thanksgiving transform into red and green, I begin dreaming of a white Christmas. Bing Crosby's classic song fills my mind and filters out over my lips with a hum. As special as it is to wake up to see the sun gleaming off of snow covered mountain peaks on Christmas morning, we must never forget that there is really only one way to have a truly white Christmas. A tragic story illustrates this point.

The story is about a young man named Lindsay, whose father was not likely to win any father-of-the-year awards. His dad was particularly distracted during the holidays. He spent much of the Christmas season on the road, and when he was home he worked long hours and had a short temper with Lindsay.

Perhaps it was the stress of the season, or perhaps it was the alcohol, but Lindsay's father was especially rough on him this time of year. Lindsay had to do extra chores on the family ranch and he endured regular whippings and verbal assaults when he did not live up to his father's expectations. He was often belittled and humiliated.

Memories of this emotional and physical abuse followed Lindsay into adulthood. Every year at Christmas, these painful recollections flooded his mind, as if demons were tormenting him and holding him captive in a prison-house of despair. One friend said, "Lindsay was never able to find happiness. He became a hard-drinking hell-raiser who went from woman to woman and couldn't find peace or success."

On December 11, 1989, at the age of 51, Lindsay listened to

Bing Crosby's "White Christmas" one last time. Then he put a gun to his head and a bullet through his brain; and that is the ironic and heartrending story of the life and death of Bing Crosby's son—Lindsay Crosby.

Lindsay once said, "I hated Christmas because of Pop, and I always will. It brings back the pain and fear I suffered as a child. And if I ever do myself in, it will be at Christmastime. That will show the world what I think of Bing Crosby's *White Christmas*."

According to the Guinness Book of World Records, Bing Crosby's *White Christmas* is the best-selling single of all time, with estimated sales in excess of 50 million copies worldwide. Nevertheless, the disheartening tale of Lindsay is a stark reminder that without Jesus to wash us whiter than snow, there can never be a genuinely white Christmas. Jesus Christ was born in Bethlehem that first Christmas morning 2,000 years ago so that our sins, though they be as scarlet, can be as white as snow.

This Christmas, as you look out the window at the gently falling snowflakes, remember the most important lesson of all: Jesus Christ was born in a manger so that He could grow up and die in your place on the cross. He rose from the dead and offers to everyone who believes in Him the free gift of eternal life. Have you trusted in Christ for salvation?

52

New Life in Christ

But God, who is rich in mercy, because of His great love with which He loved us, even when we were dead in trespasses, made us alive together with Christ-by grace you have been saved. (Ephesians 2:4–5)

* * *

I came across a humorous story recently that perfectly illustrates what Christmas is really all about. It seems a pastor was sitting in his office on the first Saturday of December. Outside in the courtyard of the church the men of the church were in the process of building a stage for a live nativity scene that would take place later in the month. It was a mild day and the pastor had his window opened, which allowed him to hear two nearby children discussing the construction project. One child asked the other, "What is this going to be?" The other child responded, "Oh, they're building a live *fertility* scene."

How perfect! A "fertility" scene indeed! According to God's Word, we are all born dead in our trespasses and sins

(Ephesians 2:10). We need to be made alive. We need new life. As Jesus told Nicodemus, we need to be "born from above." (John 3:3) It is only in Christ that we can find this new life. "Therefore, if anyone is in Christ, he is a new creation; old things have passed away; behold, all things have become new." (2 Corinthians 5:17)

When the Son of God left the eternal realm of glory, put on human flesh, and came to earth that first Christmas morning, He came to bring life. It was great news! "Then the angel said to them, 'Do not be afraid, for behold, I bring you good tidings of great joy which will be to all people. For there is born to you this day in the city of David a Savior, who is Christ the Lord.'" (Luke 2:10–11)

The Christmas story is really a fertility story. It is a story about new life. It is a story about hope for the hopeless; peace for the troubled; rest for the weary. It is a story of new beginnings and fresh starts. "But now in Christ Jesus you who once were far off have been brought near by the blood of Christ…for He Himself is our peace…." (Ephesians 2:13-14)

Jesus said, "I am the way, the Truth, and the Life." (John 14:6) He offers that life freely to all who will receive it by faith. "Come to Me, all you who labor and are heavy laden, and I will give you rest." (Matthew 11:28) Have you received the new life that only Christ offers? Have you been born again? If not let me encourage you to make this Christmas the best Christmas ever by placing your faith in the only One who can save you from the penalty of sin and give you new life. If you have already trusted Christ, and Him alone, for your eternal salvation, let me encourage you to reflect on the new life you have in Him and enjoy the abundant life that He gave you. "I come that you might have life, and that more abundantly." (John 10:10)

Merry Christmas! Have a wonderful fertility season!

WEEKLY WORDS OF LIFE

Afterword

That which was from the beginning, which we have heard, which we have seen with our eyes, which we have looked upon, and our hands have handled, concerning the Word of life—the life was manifested, and we have seen, and bear witness, and declare to you that eternal life which was with the Father and was manifested to us—that which we have seen and heard we declare to you, that you also may have fellowship with us; and truly our fellowship is with the Father and with His Son Jesus Christ. And these things we write to you that your joy may be full. (1 John 1:1–4)

* * *

I wonder what it must have been like to walk and talk with the Lord Jesus during His time on earth. For John and the other apostles, fellowship with Jesus was *real*. It was *tangible*. John wrote the words above more than sixty years after Jesus died and ascended to heaven. Yet the love and warmth of his time with Christ was still fresh in his mind even decades later. The night before Jesus was crucified, He promised His disciples that, after He was gone, the Holy Spirit would help them remember what He had taught them. Jesus said, "The Helper, the Holy Spirit, whom the Father will send in My name, He will teach you all things, and bring to your remembrance all things that

I said to you." (John 14:26) John's epistles in the Bible are the fulfillment of this promise.

Like John, we too can have fellowship with Jesus, the Word of Life, through the Holy Spirit. We can experience the assurance and joy that come with knowing Him. Even though we did not walk and talk with Him on earth, He promised to be with us always. Not long before He left this earth, Jesus reassured all believers, "Lo, I am with you always, even to the end of the age." (Matthew 28:20) I hope the devotionals in this book have helped you foster a deeper, more intimate fellowship with our Savior. I pray that this book has encouraged you to get to know our Savior even better by "holding fast the word of life." (Philippians 2:16) Moreover, like the angel told Peter and John when they were in prison, I hope these devotionals have emboldened you to "Go…and speak to the people all the words of this life." (Acts 5:20) There are many who have not believed, and the fields are "white for harvest." (John 4:25)

Perhaps you are one who has not yet believed the good news about Jesus Christ and found life in Him. If that is the case, let me encourage you to come to the only One who can give life and forgive sin. The Bible says,

> *In the beginning was the Word, and the Word was with God, and the Word was God. He was in the beginning with God. All things were made through Him, and without Him nothing was made that was made. In Him was life, and the life was the light of men. And the light shines in the darkness, and the darkness did not comprehend it. …That was the true Light which gives light to every man coming into the world. (John 1:1-5, 9)*

AFTERWORD

The light of the Gospel of Jesus Christ shines as brightly today as it did 2,000 years ago. Jesus Christ, the Son of God, died and rose again to pay your personal penalty for sin. He offers to you the free gift of forgiveness and eternal life if you will simply trust Him, and Him alone for it. Will you trust Him today? "For God did not send His Son into the world to condemn the world, but that the world through Him might be saved." (John 3:17) Jesus said, "Most assuredly, I say to you, he who believes in Me has everlasting life." (John 6:47)

WEEKLY WORDS OF LIFE

About the Author

J. B. Hixson is a nationally known author, speaker, and radio host, with more than thirty years of ministry experience in the pastoral and academic arenas. Recognized for his expertise in systematic theology, Dr. Hixson has a passion for communicating important theological truths from God's Word in a clear and easy to understand way, and for helping others learn how to study the Bible effectively for themselves. Dr. Hixson has served on the faculties and adjunct faculties of nine colleges and seminaries. He earned his B.A. degree from Houston Baptist University, Th.M. degree from Dallas Theological Seminary, and Ph.D. degree from Baptist Bible Seminary. He has authored ten books and contributed to many theological journals, magazine and newspaper articles, and other print and online media. His articles have been featured on *Harbinger's Daily*, and he is a regular guest on *Stand Up for the Truth* radio with David Fiorazo, and the *Christian Underground*

News Network podcast with Curtis Chamberlain. When he is not traveling for speaking engagements, he is in the pulpit at Plum Creek Chapel in Sedalia, CO where he serves as the Lead Pastor. J. B. and his wife Wendy have been married for thirty years and have six children and one granddaughter. For more information about Dr. Hixson, or to schedule a speaking engagement, please visit www.NotByWorks.org.

You can connect with me on:
- https://www.notbyworks.org
- https://www.notbyworks.org/store
- https://rumble.com/c/notbyworks
- https://www.youtube.com/notbyworks

Also by J.B. Hixson

J. B. Hixson is the author of ten books and hundreds of articles in theological journals, magazines, newspapers, blogs, and newsletters. His articles have been featured on *Harbinger's Daily*, and he is a regular guest on *Stand Up for the Truth* radio and the *Christian Underground News Network* podcast. To purchase books, DVDs, and other resources by Dr. Hixson, please visit NotByWorks.org.

Spirit of the Antichrist: The Gathering Cloud of Deception Vol. 1

Big Tech may censor us, but they will never silence us! In this riveting book, J.B. Hixson exposes the global elite and their Satanic conspiracy to take over the world. According to the Bible, the spirit of the Antichrist is already at work today (1 John 4:3). The entire world is under the control of the wicked one (1 John 5:19), and deception is getting worse and worse (2 Timothy 3:13). How are Satan and his Luciferian co-conspirators deceiving the world as they roll out the New World Order? Is the stage being set for the tyrannical rule of the Antichrist? In Volume One, the curtain is pulled back on the Luciferian Conspiracy. You will be introduced to realities you never knew existed and discover that lies often are hidden in plain sight.

The Great Last Days Deception: Exposing Satan's New World Order Agenda

We live in an era where "virtual reality" has replaced reality. Image trumps truth. Style supersedes substance. It has become very difficult to separate fact from fiction. This is because Satan, the prince of this world, is a liar and the father of lies. Satan, "was a murderer from the beginning, and does not stand in the truth, because there is no truth in him. When he speaks a lie, he speaks from his own resources, for he is a liar and the father of it" (John 8:44). The lies of Satan are not limited to mere theological or philosophical discussions. They have very real implications. His fabrications have swept the globe and continue to dominate the headlines of our time. These lies serve to advance his agenda in very direct ways. Even many Christians have become unwitting and unknowing captives of Satan's global deceptive scheme. How does Satan accomplish his deceptive plan today? What can we do to guard against deception? What are Satan's Top Ten Lies that most people (even Christians!) believe today? Dr. Hixson answers these and other questions in this explosive, must-have book! When we wake up to the world as it really is, it can be terrifying. Yet wake up we must if we are to survive this *Great Last Days Deception*.

What Lies Ahead: A Biblical Overview of the End Times

"One immediately noticeable quality of this book that strikes the reader is its rare combination of clarity, readability, thoroughness, and doctrinal soundness. Every major aspect of eschatology is explained in simple, practical, and understandable terms, backed by an abundance of Scripture references and thoughtful interaction. The authors have definitely accomplished their goal of writing a book suitable for both general edification and classroom use as a textbook. While the subject of eschatology may intimidate some believers, there are 30 charts and diagrams that clarify and simplify the subjects being discussed. The viewpoint represented in the book is that of traditional dispensationalism which the authors explain is simply the byproduct of a consistently literal interpretation of Scripture. As a result the authors are both thoroughly premillennial and pretribulational in their doctrinal conclusions. I highly recommend this book if you're looking for an affordable, easy-to-understand yet thorough overview of Bible prophecy that explains why God's prophetic revelation is so relevant and needed for Christians today. Maranatha!" -Tom Stegall, Grace Gospel Press

Top Ten Reasons Some People Go to Hell: And the One Reason No One Ever Has To!

"Of all of the doctrines revealed in the Bible, from humanity's perspective, soteriology, or the doctrine of salvation, would certainly be the most important since a correct understanding and response to this doctrine determines where a soul spends eternity, heaven or hell. Yet, despite its importance, the evangelical church seems to be growing progressively inaccurate and even apathetic concerning how the great salvation truths of Scripture are communicated to the lost. It is possible to miss out on a joyful eternity with God simply by misunderstanding or misconstruing the simplicity of the gospel. That is why I am delighted with this new volume written by my friend Dr. J.B. Hixson not only arguing for the simplicity of the gospel but holding forth it's truth in light of perpetual misunderstandings of it. I am always delighted to endorse Dr. Hixson's work since he is one of the few scholars who correctly understands the true grace position of Scripture and also holds to Dispensational Premillennialism. Consequently, he has the right theology necessary to rightly divide the Word of God on this critically important topic."

–Dr. Andy Woods, Pastor, Sugar Land Bible Church; President, Chafer Theological Seminary

Getting the Gospel Wrong: The Evangelical Crisis No One Is Talking About

"J. B. Hixson's book is not only the most readable, the clearest, and most concise book on what the gospel is and is not that I have read, it continues to serve as a reference work to which I return again and again. ...Hixson accomplishes a rare feat in today's theological world: he is both sharply analytical and interesting. If you want one book on the subject of the gospel which says it all and says it well, this is it!" -Dr. Mike Halsey, President, Grace Biblical Seminary, Atlanta, GA

The Gospel Unplugged: Good News Plain and Simple

"'The difference between the right word and the nearly right word,' said Mark Twain, 'is the difference between lightning and a lightning bug.' In *The Gospel Unplugged*, using clear biblical content, clever, original illustrations and refreshing certainty, Dr. Hixson reveals the difference between the gospel and the nearly right gospel, between grace and nearly grace. The distinction is important because the consequences are eternal. Thanks, Dr. Hixson, for writing a necessary book for our pluralistic culture." -Timothy K. Christian, DMin, ThD., Professor of Theology, Mid-America Baptist Theological Seminary

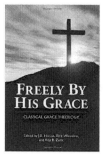

Freely By His Grace: Classical Grace Theology

Why is God's grace so amazing and important? *Freely by His Grace* provides a comprehensive survey of the many biblical facets and themes related to God's grace. It has 17 chapters plus indexes (over 500 pages) by 14 different authors presenting a classical Free Grace view. Topics covered include: the definition of Free Grace theology, the biblical theme of God's grace, the meaning of the gospel of grace, 1 Corinthians 15, Lordship Salvation, discipleship, the nature of saving faith, repentance, regeneration and the order of salvation, eternal security, assurance of salvation, sin, practical sanctification, rewards and the judgment seat of Christ, dispensationalism and its link to Free Grace, missions, evangelism, and disciple-making.

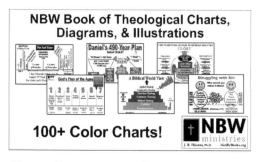

NBW Book of Theological Charts, Diagrams, and Illustrations

The *NBW Book of Theological Charts, Diagrams, & Illustrations* contains over 100 of Dr. Hixson's most requested full-color charts from his conferences and lectures across the country. These are easily duplicated on a color printer for use in your own teaching/preaching ministry.